About the Author

Robert Sommer, Professor of Psychology and Environmental Studies at the University of California at Davis, is the author of several books, including *Personal Space, Design Awareness, Expertland,* and *Tight Spaces*.

The End of Imprisonment

RECONSTRUCTION OF SOCIETY SERIES

General Editors
Robert E. Lana   Ralph L. Rosnow

JEFFREY H. GOLDSTEIN
Aggression and Crimes of Violence

ROBERT SOMMER
The End of Imprisonment

THE END OF IMPRISONMENT

ROBERT SOMMER
University of California, Davis

New York OXFORD UNIVERSITY PRESS 1976

Library of Congress Catalogue Card Number: 75-38097
Printed in the United States of America

PREFACE

I did not start out hostile to the idea of imprisonment. I first became interested in corrections as a member of a federal task force on prison architecture. At the time I believed that the problems of the prison could be solved by building small, modern institutions close to the inmate's home with ample amenities, privacy, provision for family contact, counseling, academic and vocational training, and access to community facilities. This was a liberal dream which might have worked except that it didn't take into account the obvious facts that prison is used for only a very small number of offenders in a highly discriminatory manner and that most of these offenders are losers who are marked indelibly by the experience.

Developing a program for the end of imprisonment is an ambitious undertaking; but, having witnessed the end of an era of warehousing mental patients, I do not feel it is a visionary or unrealizable objective. Fifty years ago anyone who predicted that the majority of patients would enter mental hospitals voluntarily would have been considered an idle dreamer or a candidate for commitment himself. Today we take it for granted that a majority of mental patients have signed themselves in and that the staff must ask their permission to give them drugs or electric shock, treatments which were almost entirely matters for the physician's discretion several decades ago.

The prospects for prison reform are brighter, since the target of the reform efforts is now more clearly illuminated. It is not the overcrowded facilities, the huge but always inadequate budgets, or a lack of trained personnel, although all these contribute to the problems of penal institutions, but our use of imprisonment that is the heart of the problem.

To discuss the social-psychological aspects of imprisonment, it will be necessary to attend directly to obstacles to clear thinking about crime and punishment. There have been many times when I have felt that a rational approach to issues so laden with emotion was useless. The task seems similar to writing about world federalism on a planet dominated by nationalistic rivalries. The logic of some form of world government may be obvious but the path from here to there is not. I hope to avoid this dilemma by dealing directly with the model muddle and the emotions that inhibit productive dialogue on correctional issues. Perhaps if world federalists had spent more time understanding the historical, psychological, and cultural roots of nationalism, their efforts would have been more successful. Fortunately, the reform of the penal system seems an easier task than bringing order to the chaotic international scene. There exists an appropriate recent precedent for prison reform in the case of large isolated mental hospitals, which are gradually being closed. A hundred years earlier there was a gradual termination of warehousing poor people in almshouses and children in large orphanages. The end of long-term imprisonment is organically related to the end of warehousing in other sectors.

For those who have heard all the arguments against prison, the social and psychological material may be helpful in understanding the persistence of imprisonment in the face of overwhelming evidence of its failure. The middle chapters document the fate of promising innovations in a coercive environment and the pros and cons of "good prisons" along the lines of the showcase federal facilities at Allenwood, Pennsylvania, and Lompoc, California, where several of the Watergate inmates served time. The reader who is impatient to get to solutions may turn directly to the last two chapters, which deal with the precedents, prospects, and policies for reform. This book owes much to the inspiration of two men: Humphry Osmond, a psychiatrist and friend, and Gardner Murphy, my professor and mentor over several decades. I am grateful to Harriet Becker, Nancy Russo, and Barbara Sommer, who critically read the manuscript, and to Margaret Hill for her editorial assistance. Portions of this book have appeared in modified form in the *Prison Journal,* the *Nation,* and the *New Republic*.

Davis, California R.S.
August 1975

CONTENTS

1. This Year's Prison Book, 3
2. The Model Muddle, 17
3. Obstacles to Clear Thinking, 35
4. The New Violence, 50
5. Losers Keepers, 71
6. Mock Institutions and Impersonations, 85
7. Showcase Prisons, 102
8. The Behavior Mod Scare, 121
9. Unrealized Potential of Research, 142
10. The Mental Hospital Connection, 155
11. Detention Yes, Imprisonment No, 171

Notes, 196

Index, 205

The End of Imprisonment

THIS YEAR'S PRISON BOOK

1

I know in advance that anything I have to write is either known to you already or available on the shelves of your library. I. B. SINGER

It is difficult to come up with a specific time and place for the origin of an institution as complex as the prison. Most historians credit the American Quakers of the eighteenth century with first implementing imprisonment as the major method for dealing with civil criminals. Prior to this, there had been dungeons and cells for religious, political, and civil offenders, but these were places of detention until a person's fate had been decoded. In the Anglo-Norman period of British history, major crimes were punished by execution, banishment, and mutilation, and minor crimes by fines, the pillory, or the stocks. Detention in a dungeon was not considered part of the punishment but rather a temporary expedient until the fine was paid or the penalty exacted. The places of detention built in England during the twelfth and thirteenth centuries were used mainly for debtors and political offenders. In 1552 a workhouse called The Bridewell was built in London to provide compulsory labor for beggars, vagrants, and the unemployed. Eventually such workhouses began to be used for petty offenders as well.[1]

Houses of detention were built in many parts of England and Europe over the next two centuries, but it fell to the Philadelphia Quakers to use them in an attempt to both punish and reform offenders simutaneously. At a gathering in the home of Benjamin Franklin on March 9, 1787, the Philadelphia Prison Society was formed; it lobbied successfully for the construction of the Walnut Street Jail, and eventually for penitentiaries in both Philadelphia and Pittsburgh. The Quaker advocacy of imprisonment was motivated by moral outrage at the sight of public humiliations, whippings, and executions. The idea was that the inmate, confined in a solitary cell with only the Bible to keep him company, would have time to reflect upon his misdeeds. He could see only the guard who brought his food, to whom he was not allowed to speak. This innovation received wide publicity; government officials from all over the world visited the Walnut Street Jail and later the Eastern Penitentiary. Their laudatory reports of what they saw make embarrassing reading today. Upon returning, many of the visiting officials petitioned their own governments to initiate prisons, on either the Philadelphia plan of solitary confinement or the Auburn (New York) plan of congregate living under the rule of silence. In 1812 Great Britain constructed its first penitentiary in a marshy area near the Thames River. The whole venture proved to be a disaster. Sewage was dumped directly into the Thames, and drainage of the marshy area was difficult. Within two years after the prison had been completed, an epidemic forced complete abandonment of the buildings for an entire year. The mudflats were an insufficient base for such heavy structures and buildings began to settle. The supervising architect resigned before the first building was completed and the entire venture ended up costing an astronomical sum for that time.

To find out where the American penal system went astray, it is necessary to examine its origins in the Walnut Street Jail. The Quaker notion of solitary confinement was not based on punitive desires. Rather, the Quakers viewed solitude as necessary for penitence and, even more important, as a protection against the mutual pollution of offenders. However, solitary confinement proved to be an extremely expensive way of accomplishing this, and it was inefficient in terms of industrial production. To remedy these defects the Auburn system of prison management was developed. Inmates would be allowed to congregate in the shops, the corridors, and the mess hall in silence. Both the solitary system of the Philadelphia Society and the silent system of the Auburn prison had the identical objective of reducing contact between prisoners. Two visitors from France in the early nineteenth century endorsed this principle:

> Whoever has studied the interior of prisons and the moral state of their inmates, has become convinced that communication between these persons renders their moral reformation impossible and becomes even for them the inevitable cause of an alarming corruption.
>
> . . . Absolute separation of the criminals can alone protect them from mutual pollution, and [the Philadelphia Society has] adopted the principle of separation in all its rigor.[2]

The Philadelphia and the Auburn systems were united in the objective that contact between criminals must be avoided. Once this early rationale is understood, the divergence of the present system from its origins becomes apparent. *The existing system of imprisonment isolates the inmate from contact with the outside and immerses him totally within a criminal society.* Our use of imprisonment would be abhorrent to the Philadelphia Society and to the Auburn prison officials. Instead of preventing intercourse between offenders, we are in all ways encouraging it—not only contact and conversation, but the development of a sophisticated criminal society, with a special language, prescribed roles, legends, heroes, songs, and an active economy extending into every aspect of prison life. The major resemblances between our prisons and the Walnut Street Jail are the walls, bars, and cages which now serve purposes diametrically opposite from those of the eighteenth century. The Quaker notion of solitary confinement was abandoned less because it was inhumane than for its expense and inefficiency in promoting prison industries. America accepted the substance of the Quaker idea of imprisonment without accepting the philosophy behind it. That whippings, beatings, and even executions continued to take place behind prison walls did not detract from the humane appearance of this innovation, since the brutality was removed from public view. It was this deference to community sensibilities rather than an end to corporal and capital punishment that became the hallmark of a civilized policy towards criminals.

There can be no universal ranking of punishments as to their humaneness or severity. Compared to flogging, humiliation, and exile, imprisonment may seem humane. Compared to reprimand, fines, and requiring restitution through alternative service, it doesn't. These differences in attitude reflect rather subtle cultural biases. By whose standards is it more humane to send a person to prison for five years than to place him in the stocks for a week? Public humiliation is still a common practice in socialist countries, terminating in a public confession and finally in public forgiveness. Such humiliation may be hard for the offender to take, but much less hard than several years in prison, and the forgiveness seems more genuine than what America affords its ex-convicts. Whether or not a fine will be felt as severe depends upon the offender's ability to pay. The power of exile depends on a person's feelings for his neighbors and his nation. Charles Darwin credits exile with having settled a new land (Australia) and at the same time having succeeded in the reformation of convicts better than any method known at the time.

Today the physical conditions of confinement have improved, but major criticisms of the American prison made a century ago are still valid. Today we have larger prisons and more of them, better classification of inmates—at least on paper, more attempts to separate mentally disturbed inmates, and greater recognition of the existence of women prisoners. The religious rhetoric of the past has been replaced by sociomedical jargon; but we are still trying to exorcise devils. No one can read the history of the American penal system without feeling a tremendous sense of complicity in failure. I have not found any comparable topic where the books are so universally gloomy, pessimistic, ironic, and accusatory. Major works by lawyers and penologists include *Accomplice to the Crime, The Crime of Imprisonment, The Wire Womb,* and *Prisons Under Sentence.* Books by former inmates are more lugubrious—*Frying Pan, Conversations with the Dead, The Man Died, The Devil's Front Porch, The House of Whispering Hate,* and *Castrated.* Books whose titles contain only the name of an institution arouse the same morbid images of fear and brutality. Cities adjacent to these institutions have become identified with them in the public mind. People immediately know what is meant by sending a man to Leavenworth, Joliet, or Soledad. How many of these same people know the names of institutions for the insane outside their own state borders? Nor do we yet have a prison equivalent of *Catch 22* or *One Flew over the Cuckoo's Nest* that transforms violence into absurdity.

A common method of dealing with informed critics is to bring them into the system. Once they get inside and see the problems, they either acknowledge the hopelessness of improvement and are implicated, or they leave. In the process they may succeed in getting some changes made. The main reason why co-optation has not been more widely practiced in corrections is the defensiveness towards criticism of those responsible for prisons. There is so much guilt and uncertainty that it is doubtful if a warden or prison psychologist could write an accurate account without jeopardizing his or her job. Most of the books by professionals have been written after the authors left prison service. Their books are dismissed by their former colleagues as the work of disgruntled troublemakers, as distinct from the books by outsiders, which are regarded as utopian. A candid prison official will admit the existence of violence, racism, and drug use in prison, but he feels that the reports are exaggerated. He complains that his good deeds go unrecognized while his mistakes make headlines. He will also cite attempts to eliminate abuses through better selection of guards, more training programs, new regulations, and so forth. Off the record, the same official will state bluntly that he is only doing what society has told him to do. He perceives himself as the agent of the public will. The courts have sent men to Statesville and Dannemora to be punished. If the public didn't want such places, they wouldn't exist. Correctional officials insist that they are only following the mandate of public opinion.

There isn't much political capital to be made from prison reform. It is one of those situations where the messenger gets the blame. The person who exposes brutality and corruption ultimately becomes the scapegoat. Few citizens of Arkansas were pleased when their new warden unearthed the bodies of murdered convicts in front of TV cameras. The adjacent areas where additional corpses presumably lie have still not been excavated; instead the state commissioner got rid of the new warden. The legislative branch also sets its policies according to the mandate of public opinion. Thus the task of educating the public has fallen by default to outsiders. The nation needs more busybodies like Dorothea Dix, Karl Menninger, and Jessica Mitford.

I will not repeat the innumerable incidents of brutality, corruption, and violence in prison life that have been so well documented. I am assuming that readers are familiar with the depressing record of prisons in fostering human degradation. I will also omit statistical tables and charts depicting arrest rates, convictions, parole violations, etc. Such reports are available in limitless quantities from state and federal agencies. Sadly, research in corrections has either been identified with these repetitive tabulations or with *A Clockwork Orange*. Nor will I attempt to record the history of punishment prior to imprisonment; the grisly and ever-fascinating illustrations of racks, pillories, whips, thumb-screws, gallows, and electric chairs will be omitted.

The major justification for another prison book is that the problems remain. Prisons are larger, there are more of them, there is greater violence, higher recidivism, and a rising crime rate outside. The persistence of brutality, the damage to inmates and their families, the lack of useful purpose, and the great amounts of time wasted behind bars all suggest that the problems are inherent in the institution. No one has been able to run a decent prison—not the Quakers, not the Soviets, not the conservatives or liberals, not the federal government, not the state governments, and not the counties. There is something basically wrong with the idea of forcibly removing lawbreakers from society, bringing them together in a single location, and placing them under the domination of keepers for long periods. The lives of several hundred thousand correctional employees are warped by the bad situation in which they find themselves. When I was approached to become a witness in a court suit to declare solitary confinement to be cruel and unusual punishment, it quickly became apparent that one could not attack solitary confinement and leave the mainline (i.e. the rest of the prison) intact. These prisons-within-a-prison were a special class of prison, worse in some ways than the mainline cells, but better in other respects, e.g. privacy. The logical target of a court suit had to be the deleterious effects of long-term incarceration rather than a special sort of confinement which differed only marginally from the regular cells of a maximum-security institution.

How is it that an institution that has failed so badly for so long continues in the face of criticism from every side? One explanation is that critics from the right cancel out critics from the left. Those who say prisons are too harsh are neutralized by those who say that prisons are too lenient. Those who want therapy programs are negated by those who demand more punishment. Buffeted by forces from the right and the left, the prison administrator steers a middle course and does nothing innovative. Because of their different goals, critics are not likely to unite behind any specific measure. The conjugal visiting that will weaken the prison homosexual culture is criticized as coddling convicts. Work furlough programs are attacked because they turn felons loose upon the community before they have served their full sentence. Much of this disagreement is traceable to the different goals the public has for the correctional system. Sometimes these sources of confusion are deliberately introduced to cover over a bad situation; at other times a correctional official finds himself the victim of his own rhetoric. Making public speeches about inmate gangs and hard-core offenders in order to justify a new maxi-maxi prison makes it difficult to get the community to accept furlough programs and halfway houses.

Corrections is a multi-billion-dollar industry with more than

200,000 employees working under federal, state, and local jurisdictions. It processes 2.5 million offenders annually, with over 400,000 in jails, juvenile institutions, and state prisons at any single time. The scale of the system and its expenditures are significant in view of the frequent statement that corrections is the stepchild of the criminal justice system. I am not suggesting that its budget is lavish. Prisons may be starved for funds but they are extremely expensive operations. If the billions of dollars going into corrections each year are inadequate, it is because the money is being badly allocated. More than two thirds of the offenders in the correctional system are under community supervision on probation or parole, but 80 per cent of the correctional budget goes to maintaining people in institutions and of that some 90 per cent goes to custody. The political and economic power of the institution lobby has been significant in maintaining this imbalance.

I do not care whether it is fashionable today to be a prison abolitionist. People have been calling for the elimination of prisons for 200 years without having much effect. A major reason for the failure of these past efforts was that they concentrated on reforming prisons rather than on the use of imprisonment in itself. The problems inherent in our use of imprisonment cannot be solved by building nicer prisons closer to the inmate's home equipped with single cells, more guards, counselors, and vocational educators. While such measures would be improvements over what presently exists, they would not remedy the fundamental issue which is the use of long-term incarceration as a punishment—as opposed to the *derivative* issues of prison violence, crowding, homosexuality, the quality of guards and of inmates, and the sorts of food, amenities, and "privileges" inmates should have. There is nothing glamorous about prison reform. It is a serious and depressing business. It is much easier to sell the public on more police, more jails, more guards, and stricter efforts to rid the streets of criminals.

I am deeply suspicious of any attempt to find fault with an institution by criticizing the quality of the people in it. Given the right conditions, and this includes leadership as well as resources, a failing school system or prison can be improved significantly by the people who are in it. The twin tasks of innervation and innovation may require some kind of leadership or outside assistance, but the main work of reform must be done by those most directly involved in the situation. The attempt to attribute the failure of prisons to the personalities and motives of guards and inmates will be discussed in Chapter 4 under the heading of Idealism. This doctrine tends to absolve institutions of the responsibility for failure and further stigmatizes those already fallen.

The prison is only one of many institutions in American society that are in deep trouble. An interesting experiment is to enter a bookstore and ask the clerk for "The Crisis in . . . ," letting one's voice trail off. Will the clerk bring out *Crisis in the Environment, Crisis in the American Classroom, Crisis in the Money System,* or what? A recent report on the reform of ——— described it as "a beleaguered institution . . . on the verge of collapse. Part of the problem is the new clientele being served, a bad mix of young people from inconsistent social backgrounds. . . . The pressure of these forces exhausts its strength . . . as an organized institution." Finally it is admitted that a decade of experimentation has "had very little or no lasting effect on . . . programs" and innovations have disappeared "with the departure of the charismatic promoter or with the reduction of external funding." [3] Prisons? No. This national commission was talking about high schools. In regard to ———, sociologist Amitai Etzioni writes, "If past experience is any guide, the current spate of hearings, investigating commissions and press excitation will provoke some limited legislative reforms, most of which will be quickly and easily circumvented once the mercurial spotlight of public concern turns its attention elsewhere." [4] Again the subject is not prisons, but nursing homes, a 7.5-billion-dollar industry in 1974, where the same debate about institutionalization versus community care is raging.

It may be a small consolation to prison officials to know that other institutions are being criticized, but this will not help them solve their problems. Nor is it evident to everyone that the correctional system is collapsing. The major thrust of criticism from the left is that the American penal system is becoming stronger, larger, and more securely entrenched. The search for alternatives is producing a network of new penal institutions such as the twenty-two-story space age jails in San Diego, New York, and Chicago, which may, if the history of penology is any guide, turn out to be as punitive and inhumane as those facilities they replace.

Reconstruction

When one hears government officials speak of the failure of rehabilitation, the immediate response is an ambivalence compounded of thankfulness that they have finally gotten the message and dismay that it has taken so long. One has the same mixed response to new task forces and investigations. On the one hand, they indicate recognition at a high level that something is wrong; but there is danger that the problem is being studied to death while changes occur at a snail's pace or in the wrong direction. Although the depressing history of penal reform leaves little cause for optimism, the prospects seem better now than in earlier decades. Important changes have been taking place both inside and outside prisons that cannot help but affect our use of imprisonment. There is some indication that the courts are finally, if hesitatingly, abandoning their hands-off attitude towards prisons. Tremendous amounts of money of a magnitude never seen before in corrections are available at the federal level, channeled through the Law Enforcement Assistance Administration (LEAA). At the same time, violence in institutions across the country calls attention to the failings of the system, and the closing of large outmoded mental hospitals has provided a model for closing large obsolete prisons. States such as Hawaii and Massachusetts have experimented with alternatives to incarceration which can be discussed in practical terms rather than as farfetched proposals. We have also gained, albeit at the cost of considerable human suffering, a better understanding of the seemingly hopeful innovations of past decades. Specialized institutions for different categories of offenders, like a school system with specialized placement for different ability levels, will necessarily reflect the inequalities between social classes in the larger society. Ramsey Clark at one time considered the indeterminate sentence a hopeful innovation.[5] Subsequent experience has shown, however, that inmates serve more time under the indeterminate sentence than with fixed terms. Denmark, which adopted the indeterminate sentence as a humanitarian measure, has recently repealed it. The segregation of supposedly violent offenders into specialized adjustment centers with more staff and more intensive treatment programs was also thought to be a hopeful development; but these prisons-within-a-prison turned out to be despicable places where some inmates never see daylight. We are coming to understand how a coercive environment can transform promising programs into punitive devices.

It does not seem that further documentation of corruption and brutality will contribute significantly to a long-term solution of prison problems. These accounts seem to raise the level of guilt and complicity so high that discussion ends. There is also the implication that problems can be solved by pastel-hued prisons, more money, and better-trained staff. This solution will be discussed in regards to the showcase federal prisons (Chapter 7). The record will demonstrate that although these places are far more humane than Walpole and Statesville, they are still an irrational and costly method of accomplishing society's goals. While the inmates at the nearby medium-security prison at Lewisburg are being brutalized by the unwholesome conditions of their confinement, the inmates at the minimum-security federal facility at Allenwood don't need to be there at all. It is a somewhat different brand of illogicality being practiced at Allenwood, but it remains costly, wasteful, and racist.

Dialectics

The viewpoint of this book is evolutionary and environmental. Institutions evolve over a period of time in response to the conditions in society. It is no accident that prisons have become dumping grounds for the poor, uneducated, and unskilled and for those from minority backgrounds. Nor is it accidental that the feelings and sensibilities of guards and prisoners alike are blunted in the course of their daily activities. An evolutionary view of institutions and a situational view of behavior does not preclude individual initiative or institutional reform. Reform is an evolutionary process taking place in all aspects of society. The major focus of this book will be upon the social-psychological processes underlying imprisonment and reform. In the next chapter we will discuss the impediments to clear thinking and meaningful change, which include an incredible model muddle, sugar-coated words, paleological thinking, and the tendency to reduce events to human motives. My viewpoint is that the actions of individuals are largely prescribed by the situations in which they find themselves. Those who started out in corrections as good and decent people were quickly corrupted by the system or they departed. This is not a total environmental determinism. The ranks of prison administrators have also produced some exceptional individuals; but their reforms, lacking a material and political base, were quickly eroded.

The ecologist's insistence upon interdependence does not mean that everything has to be changed at once. Rather it means that a change in one part of the system will affect all other parts of the system. To change the uses of imprisonment will necessarily affect other social institutions. However, it is not necessary to wait until all other institutions are reconstructed to change the prison system. Social institutions evolve separately within a social nexus itself in flux. Many positive innovations have occurred, including a reduction in the use of incarceration in mental hospitals, without a total overhaul of society. We are not going to be able to empty all the prisons tomorrow. On the other hand, most authorities agree that we could discharge 25 per cent of prison inmates immediately without decreasing public safety. It seems likely that another 25 per cent of prison inmates could be discharged within a year. With a continued commitment to ending the warehousing of offenders, it is probable that the long-term prison population can be reduced to 10 per cent of what it is today. At that scale we can begin to plan in practical terms for the end of imprisonment. When it comes to reform, you have to start where you are. If I were a citizen of the Soviet Union I would be approaching penal reform differently. I would spend more time on problems connected with the over-zealous application of reform and the use of medical treatment for political dissidents. I would also be more concerned about the effects of banishment (forced exile), public ridicule, and sentences that confine a person to his own district for prescribed periods. These are not among the more pressing issues facing the American penal system today.

America's jails and prisons have become the dumping grounds of people who have offended public morality. This is the same charge that was leveled aginst mental hospitals several decades ago by critics of enforced hospitalization. The mental hospital was not a totally evil institution in its day, but when it was used to put away inconvenient and ineffectual people for years, sometimes decades, the situation became intolerable. It was not merely the overcrowding, the lack of staff and treatment programs, or the occasional brutality that made the mental hospital so objectionable; it was the over-extensive use of enforced commitment to the point where the costs outweighed the benefits. To declare, as did critic Thomas Szasz, that the root of the problem was enforced hospitalization did not deny the specific problems of the institutions themselves, but rather made them derivative from the policies that got patients there in the first place.[6] Similarly, to say that the main problem with prisons is the use of imprisonment as a punishment is not to deny the very real problems faced by inmates and staff. If we can reduce our dependence upon imprisonment by realizing that caging a person for five or ten years is not humane, reformative, or inexpensive, then most of the problems of the prison can be dealt with.

The most positive comment I have heard about the prison system is that while it may be inhumane, expensive, and ineffective, it does what society wants. To the extent that this statement means that because prisons and jails exist, society must want them, it is a circular pseudo-proposition. We have come to accept imprisonment as such a natural form of punishment that it comes as a shock to realize its comparatively recent origins. The monumental solidity of prison architecture—the massive gates, the tall guntowers, the thick stone walls and steel doors—has endowed the institution with an aura of undeserved permanence. Prison administrators and their suppliers would like the public to believe that they are indispensable. There is no logical reason why this should be so. The prison is of more recent origin than other institutions such as the workhouse, the orphanage, and the almshouse which have all been abandoned in most parts of the nation. Imprisonment is a humane innovation that failed. As I hope to demonstrate, its failure was inherent within the institution itself. It is now time to admit its failure and embark upon alternative methods for handling offenders. The end of imprisonment is a realistic objective. It is more than name-changing or exorcising devils. The end of hunger in America does not mean that every citizen will go to bed well-fed every night. Rather it means that hunger on a large scale will disappear as a social problem and that no large segment will suffer continued malnutrition. The end of unemployment does not require every able-bodied person to be employed at every single moment. Rather, it means that every citizen who wants a job can find employment after a relatively short search. The end of imprisonment still leaves open the possibility of detention either for short periods or for so long as the state can prove to a jury that a person is a danger to society.

THE MODEL MUDDLE 2

"Prisons don't deter, they don't punish, they don't protect," declared the Governor. "So what the hell do they do? I think people who break the law should be punished. I have a dim view of so-called theories of rehabilitation other than enabling people to get a job. I think the idea that crime is a sickness, a disease–I don't know who thought it up 20, 30, or 50 years ago, but I don't accept it."

Our penal system is afflicted with what psychiatrist Humphry Osmond calls a model muddle.[1] Corrections employees, judges, police, legislators, and inmates all have diverse, vague, and often conflicting ideas of what prisons are supposed to accomplish. As a prominent corrections official put it, we are trying to operate the prison to be both a junkyard and a salvage yard. This has produced jarring discrepancies in the lengths of sentences, the time actually served, per capita expenditure, and the availability of counseling and vocational programs. Federal Judge Irving Kaufman circulated two hypothetical cases of criminals, along with appropriate background information, to more than forty-five federal judges in his district and asked them to recommend sentences.[2]

Case Number 1. An official of a labor union was convicted of extortionate credit dealings and related income tax violations. His prior record, narcotics use, current employment, and related matters were also included in the pre-sentence report. The sentences assigned by the judges ranged from three years' imprisonment to twenty years plus a $65,000 fine.

Case Number 2. The defendant was convicted in a jury trial of theft and possession of goods stolen from an interstate shipment. Information regarding background factors was also available to the judges. Sentences were almost evenly distributed along a continuum for four years' probation to seven and a half years in prison.

More recently the federal government undertook a larger study of sentencing practices which revealed similar inconsistencies. At the heart of the problem, Judge Kaufman believes, is basic disagreement over the goals of the criminal penalties. A judge who views imprisonment as necessary to punish a criminal, or to deter similar conduct in the future, or to isolate the offender from the community, will differ from a judge who supposes that the chief aim of confinement is reform. Judge Kaufman recommends that judges be required to state in writing their reasons behind specific sentences. This would undoubtedly get the differences out in the open for public scrutiny. However, it cannot by itself overcome the model muddle as long as judges perceive different goals for imprisonment. A successful revision of sentencing practices requires a consensus as to the objectives of punishment. We cannot continue a situation in which some judges see a prison sentence as retribution while others see it as re-education. Not only do these models have to be made explicit, but there has to be some consensus as to their appropriateness.

One way to cleave through the model muddle and the sugar-coating is to return to the original meanings of words. This is more frequently the approach of the poet than of the social scientist, who tends to conjure up hyphenated token words and use them arbitrarily. The inconsistent and arbitrary use of terms like *rehabilitation, reform,* and *punishment* has gotten us into the model muddle and euphemism has kept us there. Bogus words manufactured by committees have been used to conceal reality rather than reveal it. We will try the opposite approach and trace the words back to their original roots.

The literal meaning of *model* as an architect's plan is probably a good one for considering correctional goals. When one person is trying to build one kind of structure and another a different sort of structure, they may each accomplish their objectives *if* they are set apart and each has ample materials and space. However, if the two model builders must work cooperatively, sharing facilities and materials, without realizing that they are building different objects, the result can only be misunderstanding and mutual reproach. Models used to justify imprisonment generally affect people from beyond the focus of awareness. Although they are not often discussed explicitly, compared, or evaluated, they are the schemata which presumably underlie the day-to-day operations of the criminal justice system. I say "presumably" because so much of what occurs results from lack of a consistent model and reliance upon ad hocism or survival at any costs. When Jack Lemmon, as the businessman in the film *Save the Tiger,* was asked what he wanted out of life, he replied, "One more good season." Without workable models, the main concern becomes day-to-day survival. For guards and administrators, this means running a tight institution, staying within the budget, preventing the leakage of derogatory information, and looking after one's own people. For inmates, ad hocism means trying to survive in an oppressive situation where one's life is threatened more by other inmates than by staff and where decent food, a clean cell, a soft work assignment, and staying out of trouble become paramount goals. If fundamental change is to occur, it must be based upon the clear and consistent application of policies directed towards long-range goals. To continue with ad hocism means more of the same.

Let us examine the various models that have been used to justify imprisonment. More specifically, we ask in each case what proponents of each approach want to accomplish, whether incarceration can logically be expected to produce this result, and at what cost. I do not mean to imply that this list of models is exhaustive or irreducible. For the sake of consistency we will retain the root meaning of each term. This should help return some substance to such near-empty husks as *rehabilitation* and *reform*.

Deterrence

Deterrence has the same linguistic roots as *terror* and *tremble*, and its literal meaning is "that which frightens away from." Hence, the stronger the fear of committing an illegal act, the greater the deterrent. The fear may be of being observed, of being apprehended, of public ridicule, of punishment, or of stigma afterwards. Deterrence can operate effectively in various time frames. A white-collar criminal typically has less fear of being apprehended in the act than of being exposed afterwards. On the other hand, if someone drives a car over the posted speed limit and is not apprehended in the act, the chances of being prosecuted or punished afterwards are virtually nonexistent. Deterrence can only succeed with people afraid of the possible consequences of their actions. A person who believes there is no likelihood of being caught, prosecuted, or punished will not be deterred. Nor will deterrence succeed with someone who in the heat of passion or unreason is oblivious to the consequences of his actions or a person who calculates that the benefits of breaking the law will outweigh the disadvantages.

Deterrence is most effective when there is a certainty of quick apprehension, prosecution, and punishment. The longer any of these is delayed, the less of a deterrent there will be. Most authorities regard imprisonment as the primary deterrent in the American criminal justice system. Apart from capital punishment, it is the most severe penalty that a judge or jury can assign. Following the deterrent model, imprisonment of offenders, following conviction, should be swift and unpleasant. Presumably the more unpleasant the incarceration, either in its conditions or its length, the greater will be its deterrent value. The advocate of this model would necessarily resist attempts to improve the conditions of confinement. The country club prison and any programs for reform and re-education are antithetical to deterrence. If a person entered prison expecting to come out trained for a job, the fear of incarceration would be diminished. The counselor who wants to reform and re-educate the inmate must necessarily undermine the work of the custody employees who follow a deterrent model. Conflict between custody and treatment employees is evident in almost every American prison and can be traced back to this model muddle.

The advocates of deterrence maintain that it has not succeeded because imprisonment is applied infrequently, haphazardly, and in a discriminatory fashion. If there were better law enforcement so that a majority of criminals were apprehended and everyone convicted went to jail immediately, the deterrent value of imprisonment would be increased greatly over the present situation where most crimes are never solved and most people who are charged with offenses and plead guilty do not end up in prison. The liberal use of alternatives to incarceration has undermined its deterrent value. Some, but not all, advocates of a deterrent model would like to see longer sentences imposed. To the extent that this makes the punishment more severe, it properly belongs in this model; but when it reaches the point of ''locking them up and throwing away the key'' it belongs in the category of *incapacitation,* since its major purpose is getting the person off the streets.

Even assuming that imprisonment could be swift and sure for all convicted offenders, the high recidivism rate of released criminals raises serious questions about the effectiveness of this model.* If that small number of people who have had greatest exposure to prison are deterred seemingly *least* of all, the deterrent value of imprisonment is

* Estimates of recidivism rates vary widely from a low of 33 per cent [3] to 90 per cent [4] depending upon the type of facility and the time period during which the inmates are followed. Based on my own reading of available research, a recidivism rate of 50 per cent seems a reasonable if not a conservative estimate. In jails and other detention facilities that operate revolving doors for vagrancy, alcohol, and disorderly conduct offenders, the rate is much higher.

questionable. Discussions with ex-convicts usually reveal that jail holds no fear for them. They have been there, they know what it is, and while they would not want to return, it lacks the same frightening consequences and uncertainties it has for non-convicts. There is an old inmate saying, "If you can't do the time, don't do the crime." All too many ex-offenders without jobs or family ties feel that they have little to lose in another stay in jail. The same is true of people living in poverty and despair. The deterrent value of imprisonment is least for those people who statistically are most likely to engage in crimes against persons. This is not, however, the case with white-collar individuals, for whom a stay in jail would have disastrous consequences on livelihood, career, and reputation. Yet it is precisely this group that is sent to prison least often on the supposition that the offender has learned his lesson already, is probably able to make restitution or pay a fine, and presents no threat to the community. The deterrent model requires a greater consistency of punishment. Attempts to individualize sentences, to make them fit the life circumstances of the criminal, tend to support some model other than deterrence, presumably reform, restitution, or integration.

Rehabilitation

From the Latin meaning "to render fit again, to restore to a former status, and to reinstate," this word is related to words such as *ability* and *habit*. The prefix *re* indicates the return or restoration to something that was there before. The meaning is clear in cases of disabled soldiers (literally, those who have lost certain abilities), whose rehabilitation means a restoration to a former level through a combination of prosthetic devices, medical care, and training. The rehabilitation model implies that the former state to which one wants to return is desirable. According to this meaning, the present usage of the term in corrections makes no sense. Society would gain little from returning the inmate to the state of need, temptation, or hostility that resulted in his criminal activities. Nor do the facts of incarceration—the total immersion in a criminal society and a diminution of interest in the outside world—have any connection with a restoration to a former status. These issues will be discussed at greater length in Chapter 7; but for now, we can conclude that the rehabilitation model is either misnamed or wholly illogical. Neither the Quakers in their original conception of the penitentiary nor those who emphasize psychotherapy or punishment want a restoration to a former status. If the inmate has had a life of crime prior to his incarceration, restoration is not in society's interests, and if he has not been in a criminal society beforehand—for example, the first-time murderer—immersion in a criminal society would not lead to restoration. Whatever one assumes about the inmate's background, this model makes no sense from the standpoint either of society or of the inmate. Its demise in corrections is long overdue. Incidentally, a return to the dictionary for the meaning of rehabilitation is commonplace among inmates. The dictionary reveals the hypocrisy of official pronouncements, as well as the impossibility of accomplishing restoration under the conditions of confinement. If, under the indeterminate sentence law, an inmate is to be incarcerated until he is rehabilitated and there is no way he can be restored to his former status while in confinement, he will be kept forever. The only optimistic resolution of this Catch-22 dilemma is to conclude that the official rhetoric is false and that the authorities are keeping him locked up for some other purpose.

Having lost its original meaning, rehabilitation is stretched to mean almost anything, as in the following courtroom testimony on the effects of solitary confinement:

> Expert witness: The worst thing that these inmates have learned in the hole is, they have learned to live without needing anybody else. And if being in disciplinary confinement is totally successful, what it means is that when these men leave, if in fact they do leave, what they have learned is that they don't need anybody else.
>
> Judge: Let me ask you something. Are you inferring they learned self-reliance?
>
> Expert witness: Oh, yes, that they learned a kind of self-reliance—not the kind that Emerson was talking about, but the kind. . .

> Judge: Well, isn't the whole purpose of rehabilitation to bring about a feeling and the ability to rely on one's self? Isn't self-reliance one of the very functions of rehabilitation? [5]

Reform (*Corrections*)

Literally, to reform is "to reshape, form again, or change into a new and improved condition." Its concrete realization, the reformatory, had as its goal the reshaping of a young person's character. Although the term has rather archaic overtones, this is what most advocates of rehabilitation really want. Rather than restoring a person to a former status, either as someone desperately in need of money or full of hatred, the goal of the reformer is to reshape the offender into a new and improved form.

This model is the logical antecedent of today's emphasis on *corrections,* literally "a setting right or on a straight path." John Augustus, the first probation officer, wrote in 1852 that "the object of the law is to reform criminals, and to prevent crime and not to punish maliciously, or from a spirit of revenge." [6] This eminently sensible view led Augustus to bail offenders out of prison and keep them in his home. Unfortunately, the term *reform* subsequently became associated with such brutal institutions as the reform school and state reformatory, so it became lost to the criminal justice system and a less useful term (rehabilitation) was substituted. However, the attempt at euphemism was only partial. We still talk about reforming prisons when we want to change them. To rehabilitate prisons, at least in common speech, would mean refurbishing or modernizing older facilities. Both reform and corrections emphasize a reshaping, and corrections has the additional connotation of a standard to guide the process of change—setting the person not just on a different path, but on the right path. Most inmates will acknowledge the legitimacy of reform as a social objective, whereas rehabilitation makes no sense to them. Their criticisms concern the practicability of accomplishing positive character change through immersion in a total criminal society; any reforming or reshaping under such circumstances would probably be in a negative direction. Ironically, *reform* today is more often applied to efforts to change institutions than to programs to change prisoners.

Retribution (Vengeance)

Meaning "to pay back or return," retribution is interpreted as society "paying back" the offender for his misdeeds through some form of punishment or conversely, the offender repaying society through his pain and suffering. The deep emotional roots of retribution will be examined more fully in the discussion of paleologic. Our immediate association to vengeance is an eye for an eye, a tooth for a tooth, and society exacting its pound of flesh from the criminal. In ancient times the family or tribe of a dead person would revenge themselves upon the murderer, whose own family or tribe could be expected to defend him. Blood revenge was the religious duty of the next of kin, who did not so much hate the killer as he feared the ghost of the killed who demanded the blood of the murderer before he could lie in peace. Blood revenge began terrible feuds between families and cities that persisted for generations. The debilitating effects of this escalated retribution led to the system under which blood money was accepted as payment for homicide and other crimes. The authority to exact vengeance was removed from the individual and family and given to the state. The adaptive value of this change in reducing violence among citizens and between families and states is evident. However, it established the basis for a retribution model in which the state supplants the victim in taking revenge.

Prisons in Singapore still employ flogging with certain classes of criminals. According to prison director Quek Shi Lei, offenders convicted of crimes against persons, such as robbery, assault, and muggings, are flogged "in such a way that criminals will get a taste of the violence they inflict on their victims . . . and the punishment is intended to leave scars on the criminal for the rest of his life." [7] Several American prisons use flogging as a disciplinary tool within the institution but not as a punishment for a crime committed on the outside.

Adherents of retribution are particularly exercised by the diversity of sentencing practices from one courtroom to the next and the use of the indeterminate sentence. Any variation in the type or length of punishment for offenders convicted of the same crime undermines the retribution model which seeks an eye for an eye, not a tap on the wrist for one offender and twenty lashes for the next. It is also difficult to apply this model to victimless crimes such as drunkenness, drug use, and morals violations which constitute the major portion of arrests throughout the nation. We arrest people for homosexual offenses and place them in a prison situation where homosexuality is either tacitly accepted or openly practiced. We place drug offenders in a prison environment where drugs are more readily available than they are outside. This is particularly true of tranquilizers and downers which flow in a torrent down the tiers to keep things quiet.

Among inmates there is a high degree of acceptance of the retribution model in its ideal form. Inmates object to the discriminatory fashion in which it is applied and the hypocrisy of concealing it under sugar-coated terms like corrections, rehabilitation, and reform. The thirst for revenge is not easily eliminated, but it can be controlled by rational self-interest. The transfer of punishment from the victim to the state and the change from a literal application of an eye for an eye to symbolic equivalents are fundamental alterations in the classic retribution model. They suggest that further alterations of this approach are possible.

Retribution has a special cathartic significance for the offender, who believes that once he has paid his debt to society the slate should be wiped clean. He should be able to start a new life without stigma, since he "has already paid." The legal discrimination against ex-convicts, the loss of civil rights, and frequent harassment by authorities undermine the legitimacy of retributive punishment. However, the most serious problem with this model is the difficulty in developing symbolic equivalencies for the vast array of criminal offenses ranging from perjury to smoking a marijuana cigarette. Finally, the retribution model puts all its emphasis upon punishing the offender and ignores the victim.

Restitution

To restitute means "to restore, replace, or set up again"; restitution gets the victim back into the picture. Offenders are expected to repay any money stolen or repair any damages inflicted. This model cannot be applied literally in capital offenses or when bodily harm has been inflicted or in victimless crimes. In such instances, money or service becomes the symbolic equivalent of direct repayment. Such a system is used in accident cases, where a victim might receive $5000 for the loss of an arm, $20,000 for blindness, etc. Socialist countries employ the rhetoric of restitution in demanding labor for the state as a penalty for crimes against the state. However, since an inmate can be discharged from a labor camp once he is considered reformed or ideologically pure, re-education and deterrence seem the primary objectives and restitution a secondary consideration.

Restitution and deterrence are sometimes combined in sentencing white-collar criminals. An embezzler may be ordered to make full restitution *and* pay a penalty either to the state or to the victim. The penalty can be interpreted as either restitution for mental suffering or as a punitive deterrent to others who might be similarly tempted. Repayment of victims is central to what historian David Rothman calls a *failure model,* in which society recognizes its "inability to achieve such heady and grandiose goals as eliminating crime and remaking the offender."[8] Rothman provides several examples of the way society has acknowledged failure in other areas and dealt with it rationally. The businessman who has failed can declare bankruptcy and pay off his creditors in depreciated currency. The court permits him to settle his debts at ten cents on the dollar. Introducing this concept into corrections would mean allowing the inmate to pay off his debt to society in depreciated currency, specifically in shorter sentences rather than the inflated terms that now prevail. Society deals with fires and other natural catastrophies through a series of preventive measures and insurance coverage. Home owners and business people carry fire insurance, not as a cure for fire but to protect themselves against loss. Federal crime insurance would not eliminate crime, but would make its effects less burdensome. At present, the victim of an assault is most likely to receive nothing. Society spends a great deal of money trying to catch the criminal, put him on trial, and then incarcerate him. Admitting the failure, at least of the incarceration, would permit some of the money to be diverted to the victims of crime. Money cannot bring back a person killed by a mugger, but it can make life easier for the dead person's family. New Zealand and Great Britain, as well as eleven American states, have programs for reimbursing victims of violent crime based on the proposition that when the government fails in its obligation to protect its citizens, it should at least help compensate them for their losses.

Several American cities are experimenting with repayment of society through community service. County judges in Portland, Oregon, have the option of channeling consenting offenders into any of more than 200 cooperating service agencies. Part-time jobs are scheduled so that they do not conflict with the offender's regular employment. During the first year, more than a thousand offenders participated, and this number has increased. The offenders prefer spending time in productive community service instead of simply "putting in time" in jail. Offenders without special skills may do menial labor in the park or in convalescent hospitals, while skilled offenders perform their regular work in a public service context. A physician may be required to provide medical treatment for skid row alcoholics, or a plumber to help renovate dilapidated buildings.

Considering the harmful effects of long-term incarceration, it is not illogical to develop some form of restitution program for inmates themselves. Payment would come in the form of special education and job training benefits, opportunities for medical treatment and counseling, and subsidies for living in halfway houses. Such assistance would be more meaningful to the inmate who has been discultured and desocialized after a long stay behind bars, and would be far more effective in reducing recidivisim, than adding meaningless educational and vocational programs to existing prisons. Similar proposals for helping offenders were made several centuries ago by Beccaria and Jeremy Bentham, but they have rarely been implemented.

Incapacitation

Meaning "the state of being held in or contained," *incapacitation* has relatively neutral emotional connotations. The model has also been described as *detention,* meaning "being held back or down." Nothing is said about how long a person is held or under what circumstances. Applied to imprisonment, the model has meant the physical removal of the offender from society, but incapacitation can also cover chemical and surgical means of restraint. Capital punishment is more than a containing operation, but it is an extreme way of accomplishing the same results. Less obvious measures include loss of vocational licenses, deportation, and to some extent confiscatory fines leveled against those whose crimes require a supply of capital.[9] In the pure application of incapacitation, no effort is made to change the person detained or punish her further. This accords with the oft-heard proposition that criminals are in jail to remove them from circulation and not to be punished. In other institutions that contain the mentally retarded or senile, the incapacitation is done purportedly for the person's own good. The once-common procedure of putting debtors in prison was intended to keep them from incurring further debts as well as to hold them until repayment was made.

The major weakness of this approach is its vagueness as to the circumstances and length of incapacitation, its disruptive effects on a person's life, the corrosive influence of the wrong kind of confinement, and the expense. Incapacitation has meant everything from life imprisonment (lock them up and throw away the key) to the forced relocation of Japanese-Americans in concentration camps during the Second World War. In the latter case there was no evidence that Japanese-Americans were disloyal, and many young Nisei were allowed to leave the concentration camps to join the American army. The government's justification was that the Japanese on the West Coast were potential spies and saboteurs. The relocation went beyond mere geographic removal (exile) since the Japanese-Americans were confined in concentration camps surrounded by barbed wire and machine-gun posts. The camps had a minimum of amenities and were in desolate locations. Families were left intact, but family roles were altered. The men had little productive occupation in the deadening camp routine. Confinement was oppressive and disruptive to the inmates even though there was very little direct brutality from the American soldiers who served as guards. After the war, many of the released inmates found themselves unable to return to their homes and pick up their former lives where they had left them. These internment camps illustrate the negative side of incapacitation. Even if the camps had been better outfitted and located in more attractive settings, the basis of the incapacitation would have required security (armed guards) and a mind-deadening institutional routine. There is no way of detaining people against their will for years without doing them injury. In cases where people's lives are disrupted for the social good, such as for army service, the government sees fit to compensate them with bonuses and educational benefits which are tied directly to the length of service.

For the criminal justice system, the key question regarding incapacitation is its length. If a person poses a threat to society in 1975, is there any justification for turning him loose in 1978 or 1984, particularly since his anti-social attitudes are likely to worsen during continued confinement? Potential life sentences have not succeeded in preventing crimes within the prison itself. Every American prison is a hotbed of illegal activities, with much higher rates of robbery, assault, rape, and drug abuse than in the society outside. Nor does there seem an effective method for gauging potential actions after release from the limited range of behaviors distorted in the unnatural milieu of the prison. Since the incapacitation model provides no basis for deciding when the inmate is to be released, incapacitation either has to be forever or be supplemented by another model such as deterrence, retribution, or reform.

Re-education

This model brings out most clearly the difference between the goals of the penal system in the United States and in socialist countries. Most American prisons have education departments which are concerned with providing basic academic and vocational skills. *Re-educate,* literally meaning "to bring out again," refers to redirecting an educational process that went wrong somewhere. The term has fallen into bad company; it is identified today with scare words such as *indoctrination, brainwashing,* and *behavior modification.* According to the American ethic, teaching skills is acceptable, brainwashing isn't. The distinction has deep roots in the American attitude towards all service institutions. The fear of the state embarking upon programs to change attitudes and behavior is understandable in a democracy whose citizens are supposed to elect those who determine state policy. If the policymakers can control the minds of the populace, then the whole conception of democracy becomes tautological, with those in power using their authority to shape attitudes that will insure their continued control. Attitude change as government policy at any level is righly feared in a democratic system, even in corrections.

In the Soviet Union, political education accompanies imprisonment, and re-education is virtually synonymous with reform. Offenders are told of the political significance of their transgressions and made to understand the necessity of changing their ideas. A Soviet guard would *not* give the advice to new inmates so commonly heard in American prisons, "Do your own time and you'll get out of here." Rather, the offender would be advised to express positive attitudes and cooperate in his own rehabilitation as a means of getting out. This will mean defining his crime in political terms, i.e. robbery is considered anti-social. This brings us directly to another specific goal of punishment in socialist countries—*repentance,* meaning the feeling of remorse over one's misdeeds. In practice this means securing a detailed confession from an offender, not only to make the person feel sorry and apologize publicly, but to use the confession as an ideological weapon. It frequently happens that after a person has confessed, the state has no further use for him and he may be released depending upon the whim of his captors.

Forced confession and political indoctrination are abhorrent to the American system, even for prison inmates. The reasons behind this are both practical and ideological. Confessions from people in a coercive environment are given little credence by the courts. Indoctrination is strongly resisted by prisoners, as expressed in a recent statement by a prison movement leader: "Lock me up, but leave my head alone." Unfortunately, this view embodies a logical contradiction. There is no way of removing a person from society and locking him up without affecting his head. The critical issue is not whether a change will occur in the prison environment, but whether there is to be a conscious attempt to change attitudes and behaviors in a socially prescribed direction rather than leaving this to the vicissitudes of the prison milieu; this will be discussed more fully in a later chapter on behavior modification. Senator Ervin, whose Senate committee spent considerable time investigating behavior modification, warned that "the most serious threat posed by the technology of behavior modification is the power this technology gives one man to impose his views and values on another. . . . If our society is to remain free, one man must not be empowered to change another man's personality. . . ." [10]

The federal government has just begun a program in which inmates from several California prisons have been "furloughed" to a branch of the University of California. They live near campus in supervised apartments and follow strict rules regarding curfew and off-campus trips. While it has been commonplace for prisons to allow selected inmates to enroll in correspondence courses and occasionally to attend a college course during the day, this program represents a significant federal commitment to a non-coercive albeit institutional alternative to imprisonment. The cost of tuition and living expenses ($270 a month) is significantly less than that of keeping an offender in a federal prison. At the end of the program the participants will emerge with college degrees. So far there have been no runaways, crimes committed, or major rule infractions, although everyone is keeping his fingers crossed. Faculty consider participants to be "model students," which is not surprising in view of their motivation to stay out of prison. While at university, these offenders receive no special indoctrination or sermonizing other than that given to ordinary students.[11] Programs like this which give straightforward education, either academic or vocational, are non-contentious, as distinct from political re-education which, at least in socialist countries, is very close to a reform model.

Integration

This is the newest token word among correctional officials. It is at the heart of community corrections, which puts an emphasis on keeping the offender's ties with the community intact during the time he is being punished. *Integrated,* literally meaning "whole, entire, or intact," has the Latin roots *in* (not) and *tag* (to be touched). Applied to corrections, it means that the offender's social, vocational, and family ties are "not to be touched" adversely by the punishment itself. This can be best accomplished, according to this model, by keeping the offender out of the cesspool and keeping him in a healthy community. Integration can therefore be seen as a policy of minimizing the negative consequences of imprisonment (isolation, loss of social and vocational skills, family disruption) while still preserving deterrence and retribution. Examples of the integration model are the programs developed in Iowa for keeping offenders in the community where they can make restitution rather than incarcerating them, or the California program in which the state pays counties for keeping youthful offenders on supervised probation in their own communities rather than sending them to state facilities.

This model is inadequate in cases where the individual was poorly integrated into the community prior to his crime or when the community itself has disintegrated. Integration as a goal of punishment makes no sense for an habitual prostitute whose outside associations were totally within a criminal culture. Nor can ties be established with a community that does not exist or want the offender back. Viewing the community as an instrument of reform implies that there is a community in reasonably good shape that is willing and able to undertake the task of reforming offenders. None of these assumptions seems tenable in regard to most prison inmates. Those areas contributing the largest number of offenders have more problems than they can handle already and the least resources with which to handle them. Another example of the way in which our words trap us into applying unrealistic models is our use of *ghetto* and *barrio* as if these were genuine neighborhoods dedicated to taking care of their own people and maintaining public services. Sometimes they are, but often they are merely geographic locations without internal social cohesion or workable institutions for handling their problems.

Postscript

In practice there will always be overlaps between different correctional models. Most programs will involve several goals. For example, a community service program may be based on deterrence plus restitution plus integration. Failure to distinguish clearly between models will result in hypocritical rhetoric and unobtainable objectives. Use of more than one model is possible, but contradictory aspects must be resolved if desired goals are to be achieved.

OBSTACLES TO CLEAR THINKING 3

Paleologic

> *I will give up my gun when they peel my cold dead fingers from around it.*
> BUMPER STICKER

> *A crate of guns is far deadlier than a crate of dynamite.*
> NEW YORK POLICE CHIEF PATRICK V. MURPHY

We are accustomed to people explaining their actions on the basis of rational self-interest. This expectation is usually confirmed, since there can be a logical justification for anything, including war, suicide, and sexual abstinence. Yet sometimes it seems that the arguments are more rationalization than reason. There are many paths to the truth—some people follow religion, others poetry, politics, or the law. Each seeker starts out with his own key assumptions and proceeds from there to his own conclusions. A poet's rules of evidence are very different from those of a lawyer or biologist. The poet's simile of falling leaves and human frailty has no standing in the courtroom; and a dummy corporation designed to transfer assets on a single occasion, which seems to most people to be a legal fiction and subterfuge, has a very tangible existence for a businessman.

Silvano Arieti, a psychiatrist who has devoted his life to working with schizophrenics, coined the term *paleologic* to describe patterns of thinking that are primitive, emotionally laden, and outside ordinary rational constraints.[1] Myth, legend, and fantasy often follow paleologic. Children use it liberally at certain stages of their intellectual development. The term *paleological* seems preferable to either *irrational* or *illogical,* which both suggest an absence of logic. Paleologic has its own rules and, in the case of children's thinking, is highly predictable. Experiments have shown that a child up to a certain age believes that a tall thin glass contains more liquid than a short wide glass, even though the child has observed the same amount of liquid being poured into both glasses. From the standpoint of adult thinking this is paleologic, even though to most children below a certain age this response is perfectly natural. Adelson studied the development of ideas of crime and punishment among adolescents of all social classes in three nations, the United States, West Germany, and Great Britain.[2] He found that neither intelligence, sex, nor social class counted as much in the development of moral concepts as age. There is a profound shift in the character of the child's moral thinking which occurs at the onset of adolescence (age 12–13), and is essentially completed by the time the child reaches 15 or 16. Some children develop earlier or later than others, but Adelson is describing developmental trends such as an increase in abstract thinking that occurs between early and middle adolescence. When twelve- and thirteen-year-olds were asked, "What is the purpose of laws?" they replied:

> They do it, like in schools, so that people don't get hurt.
> If we had no laws, people could go around killing people.
> So people don't kill or steal.

Replies from fifteen- and sixteen-year-olds were more abstract:

> To ensure safety and enforce the government.
> To limit what people can do.

> They are basically guidelines for people. I mean, like this is wrong and this is right and to help them understand.

For the early adolescent the process and institutions of society are personalized. When asked about the law, a youngster talks about the policeman, the judge, and the criminal, while the older adolescent employs notions of community, authority, rights, liberty, and equity. Increasing maturity also produces an extension of time perspective and a tolerance for complexity. When presented with the problem of recidivism, younger adolescents talk mainly about further punishment: "Well, they don't know anything, and you have to teach them a lesson," or, "Because they want to go back to prison. They are used to it and their friends are there." To a varied set of questions on crime and punishment, the youngsters consistently proposed one form of solution: punish, and if that does not suffice, punish harder: "Well, these people who are in jail for about five years and are still on the same grudge, then I would put them in for triple or double the time. I think they would learn their lesson then."

At maturity the time perspective of the early adolescent lengthens, and issues which could previously only be dealt with in the most primitive way are the subject of rational thought and discourse. This doesn't occur in one hundred per cent of the cases because some individuals remain at their early level of conceptualization or some degree of it. Societies also develop and mature, and issues that are covered with emotion and unreason at one period can be discussed rationally later; there is some indication that rational public dialogue on marijuana laws is finally possible. Attitudes imbued with paleologic are found at all ends of the political spectrum. Ecological awareness, the respect for all living creatures, goes beyond rational self-interest into deeply rooted emotional impulses. Even though one can make a good rational argument for an ecological perspective, the case for saving the Death Valley pupfish or the blue whale is basically a matter of faith. Arguments pro and con can be fully rational, but behind them lie unverifiable emotionally charged assumptions about the purpose of life. Attitudes towards the flag, towards parental authority, towards the law, and towards the preservation of a historical building—all these are deeply imbued with paleologic. An unscrupulous politician manipulates paleologic in order to sway public opinion, using catch words and slogans that ignore the complexity of issues.

A reliance on paleologic is one of the main factors that can be used to differentiate between the retribution and restitution approaches to punishment. Retribution looks back at the crime and demands emotional satisfaction, proof that the criminal has paid. Restitution puts emphasis on repayment of the victim regardless of whether or not one is able to punish the assailant. Restitution does not have the same paleological quality as vengeance. When we see a newspaper photograph of a convicted burglar sweeping the sidewalk at the Portland City Zoo, the immediate response is that the person may not be suffering enough, even though we realize that this work is probably more beneficial to society and less harmful to the individual and his family than his serving time in the state penitentiary. When a judge sentences an inmate to five years "at hard labor," this is usually a sop to the retribution model. The judge has no idea of whether or not the convict's future work assignment will be hard or soft.

It is difficult even for a psychologist to specify what is so satisfying about "an eye for an eye, a tooth for a tooth." The desire for vengeance upon the lawbreaker is not often discussed productively. People become threatened, upset, and angry when retribution is mentioned. The inherent conflict with notions of love, charity, and humanity, also heavily endowed with paleologic, inhibits meaningful discussion. Attitudes toward capital punishment and gun ownership are similarly fraught with paleologic. There are valid arguments pro and con on both issues. Not every defense of capital punishment is irrational or immoral. The opposite belief that all human life is sacred regardless of circumstances, including that of terminal illness, is based on paleologic. Knowing this can help us understand the terrible acrimony and frustration accompanying discussion of serious correctional issues. The model muddle can account for the confusion, but understanding the acrimony requires us to attend to paleologic.

The hostility often directed towards the penal reformer has deep roots in blood revenge. In many places and times it has been a crime to intercede on behalf of a convicted offender. In ancient Greece, a condemned man was not allowed to present a petition for pardon, nor was any individual citizen allowed to do so in his behalf. A citizen of the town of Nuremberg in 1482 could be fined and receive even harsher penalties if he dared to ask "princes, counts, wards, prelates, and other persons of high rank" to intercede on behalf of a criminal.[3] Interestingly enough this prohibition did not apply to preaching monks, barefooted friars, lepers, and foundlings. The categories exempted would appear to many people as the counterparts of today's prison reformers.

Knowing the origins of a person's beliefs is indispensable for productive discussion even when one does not share those beliefs. Much of our understanding of crime and punishment is beyond rational discourse. I can only grasp partially what rape means to a woman. My understanding is somewhat diffuse and inchoate, but it alerts me to the hypersensitivity of women on issues whose significance is only dimly perceptible to me. Discussion with a woman who has been raped will be painful for both of us, at least in the beginning. But in dealing with paleologic there is no substitute for getting feelings out into the open and confronting them directly. This means working through the defenses that inevitably arise. Many people are ashamed to admit holding the retribution model, even though it strongly colors their views of how offenders should be treated. Religious precepts as well as politeness keep vengeance from percolating to the surface except in times of stress. Public attitudes that are steeped in paleologic cannot be changed directly through rational argument. Something more is required, and this is the leaching process to drain away the paleologic.

Anyone writing about correctional issues must consider the value of an intellectual approach in a situation where so much lies beneath the surface. Criticizing imprisonment on rational grounds is similar to developing plans for world government on a planet dominated by nationalistic passions. Yet it is critical to consider issues, even though the prospects for reform are remote at the particular time. Advocates of world government might have been more effective if they had dealt directly with the unconscious psychological aspects of nationalism. Whatever else it accomplishes, public discussion of correctional issues will help to drain away the emotional charge. Hopefully, there will come a time not too distant when reasoned discussion of imprisonment will be possible without tripping over slogans about "coddling convicts," "rehabilitation not punishment," and "an eye for an eye, a tooth for a tooth." Any one of these positions can be logically defended, but until the paleologic percolates to the surface and is dealt with, rational discussion is not going to occur. Given a topic as complex and emotionally charged as punishment for lawbreakers, which is at the heart of religion and morality, one cannot expect perfect agreement among citizens. There will always be a dynamic tension in this area pulling toward either severity or leniency.

While most discussion of penal issues emphasizes differences between opposing positions, there is virtual unanimity on several major objectives of a criminal justice system, such as protecting society, deterring criminals, and providing offenders with educational and vocational skills. This agreement among prison officials and prison abolitionists can serve as a basis for constructive dialogue. More than any other institution, the judiciary has been best able to handle emotional issues on a rational basis. The court chamber and its elaborate rituals, the dignity of the proceedings, and the isolation of judge and jury are designed to encourage rational consideration. The judge will explicitly tell the jury to refrain from thinking about the punishment and consider only the guilt or innocence of the defendant, as in these instructions in a celebrated case:

> You are instructed that the question of possible punishment of the defendants in the event of conviction is of no concern of the jury, and should not in any sense enter into or influence your deliberations. . . . You cannot allow a consideration of the punishment which may be inflicted upon the defendants to influence your verdict in any way.[4]

With more general social issues such as penal reform or gun control, where the electorate rather than a sequestered jury must make the decisions, the reduction of paleologic can be likened to the process of *systematic desensitization,* a therapeutic technique developed by Joseph Wolpe.[5] According to Wolpe, every time a person is exposed to a frightening object without any fearful consequences occurring, the linkage between the object and the fear is reduced. Therapy sessions consist of a planned program of adaptation to a feared object under conditions where the threat of danger is minimal. The young man who is afraid of snakes would first be asked to write down a list of items connected with snakes in a numerical order of increasing fear. This list, called his *anxiety hierarchy,* might put "Reading the word 'snake' " at the top of the list (not very fearful), "Gazing at a plastic model of a snake" somewhere in the middle, and "Handling a live snake" at the bottom (most feared) of the list. Next the young man would be trained to relax through breathing exercises, meditation, and pleasant visual imagery.

Therapy begins with the least feared situation. The young man would look at the card with the word "Snake" printed on it until he declares without qualification that he can hold the card in his hand and still feel relaxed. Wolpe then proceeds to the second item, perhaps a drawing of a snake, again waits until the young man can honestly say that he can look at the drawing and still feel relaxed. Incidentally, nothing terrible is happening to the young man at this time, so it is perfectly natural for him to be unafraid of the drawing. However, each exposure to snake-related objects weakens the fear bond surrounding snakes. Soon the therapist gets to the point where the young man can hold a plastic model of a snake in his hand and report feeling relaxed. If at any time the patient says that he is not comfortable, he returns to the relaxation exercises until the tension disappears and can proceed. These methods have proven effective in diminishing various phobias.

Desensitization means taking bad-tasting medicine in very small doses so that the person adapts to it. Supreme Court decisions follow the same kind of pattern. Rarely does a decision spring full-bloom from a single case. Actually, the Supreme Court does not usually take a case until it has been decided in a series of lower courts, a process which in itself has desensitizing qualities. Every time an issue gets into public notice, some of the paleologic drains away, even when the controversy itself swirls furiously. This intense reaction is often a necessary accompaniment to the eventual dissipation of the paleologic. Those who were so passionate in their opposition to abortion assisted in the process of draining the emotion from the issue. This does not mean that all problems connected with legal abortion have been solved, but rather that the topic can now be discussed rationally, something which could not be done fifty years ago. It seems likely that such catharsis and conflict will be necessary before Americans can come to terms with capital punishment, gun ownership, heroin maintenance, and many other issues of direct concern to the criminal justice system. When the heat goes out of the argument, people will be in a better position to use the light. This has probably happened already in the case of possession of marijuana, even though the arrest figures in 1974 did not reflect it. The intense feeling and revulsion produced by any attempt to reduce penalties on marijuana has dissipated. The legislatures may not come around to legalizing marijuana, but they will be in a position to engage in rational discussion as a precursor to developing rational policies. One should not be too impatient even when the dialogue never seems to progress beyond name-calling or a litany of familiar arguments. Like the accident victim who is obsessed with the retelling of his tale, the constant repetition draws out the emotional charge until finally the story can be told without tears and trembling.

Euphemism

> *We Yankees think we can change problems by changing the name of the problem.* CHARLES MC CABE

I visited three prisons in the course of two busy weeks; one was officially named a Facility, another a Camp, and a third a Colony. The similarities between the three institutions were more apparent than the minor differences. The renaming of all but two California prisons took place over a decade ago, but colloquial speech has remained remarkably unaffected. In referring to prisons, most people use the city name or initials; Duell Vocational Institute is DVI or "Tracy," the city closest to the institution. The motives for euphemism are readily apparent in the case of prisons. When something isn't working well, it is easier to rename it than fix it. Changes in terminology are inexpensive, quick, and painless, while tangible reforms are time-consuming, expensive, and painful. The prison business is not alone in using euphemism. Government bureaus in the 1970s were instructed to eliminate the word *poverty* from official documents and substitute *low-income.* The term *slum* was replaced by *inner city,* and for *black, brown,* or *minority status,* read *community people.* An American officer serving in the Mekong Delta region of Vietnam described how he was instructed first to write "search and destroy" on operational plans, then after two months "search and clear," and finally "reconnaissance in force," when in fact it was always the same operation. Today there is a determined effort to replace the term *parole* with a sweeter-sounding word. A proposed revision of the California Sentencing Code discards the use of *parole* entirely:

> Confusion between the words "parole" and "probation" has been annoying to both professionals and laymen, and further, the terms "parole" and "parolee" are more pejorative in the public mind than "probation" and "probationer." Under the new system all offenders under community supervision are simply *probationers.*[6]

My views about name-changing parallel those of psychiatrist Henry Davidson in his article "Psychiatry and the Euphemistic Delusion."[7] No matter what the dictionary says, or what is conjured up in our conferences or committees, it is the word in operation which counts. When something is good, its name doesn't need changing, and if it is bad, it is dishonest and futile to invent a new term. The true meaning always wears through the verbal varnish. If a decent warden and staff can turn the state prison at Walla Walla, Washington, into a humane institution, it doesn't matter whether Walla Walla sounds funny and "prison" sounds medieval. New names are supposed to reflect new program emphases. If this represents a major overhaul, then the change may be warranted. However, the addition of a single program in a large institution does not warrant a shift in terminology. An analogy would be renaming Missouri University "The Missouri Communications University" because the university happens to have a strong school of journalism. Even though the J School may be excellent, most of the students at the university are not enrolled in journalism courses.

The colloquial speech of most inmates and guards ignores the sugarcoating. There are cons and screws, ballbusters and bastards, low riders, dudes, and punks. Even the children of the guards take on prison argot. This is an international language which has existed for centuries. Books about prisons frequently contain glossaries defining special terms. Guards in the United States and England have for centuries been called *screws.* One source traces the term back to *turnkey,* with *screw* meaning *key.* Another traces its origins to the thumbscrew, a device used by guards to obtain confessions from prisoners. There are local and ethnic variations of prison argot. California prisoners use an amalgam of terms from the drug culture, ethnic communities, and older criminal slang. Local conditions may produce idiosyncratic usage. The gallows at the state prison in Leavenworth, Kansas, was kept in a storehouse. When a man was brought there to be hanged, the other inmates described this as "gone to the corner" or "paying a visit to the warehouse." Elsewhere inmates referred to the gallows as "the dancehall" and hanging as "dancing on air." With the end of hanging, such expressions have become vestigial parts of the prison culture.

Prison argot is the very opposite of euphemism, which is intended to conceal meaning and to scatter pleasant incense over rot and decay. Convicts' speech is direct, descriptive, and packed with imagery. Con language is part of the initiation ceremonies within the inmate culture. It serves to subjugate individuality and convey the lesson that prison is a special world whose local rules and customs must be heeded. Prison argot is not a code system for concealing communication since everyone in prison—guards, the warden, and even the chaplain—is familiar with it. It also has a desensitizing function in draining paleologic from the convict's situation. Most convicts are able to discuss their imprisonment in rational terms. They may be bitter and resentful of their situation, but their perceptions of the immediate environment are accurate.

There are two divergent views about the need for cleaning up language. George Orwell stated, "The present political chaos is connected with the decay of language and one can possibly bring about some improvement by starting at the verbal end." [8] Orwell believed that the rhetoric of all political parties, from the far left to the far right, and including all points in between, is "designed to make lies sound truthful and murder respectable and to give an appearance of solidity to pure wind." He felt that people would have to clean up their language before they could clean up their thinking and actions.

The tendency to euphemism is not true of all people. Psychiatrist Humphry Osmond points out that the blind still prefer to be called blind rather than poor-sighted or by some other euphemism.[9] The acceptance of a clear descriptive label often indicates a willingness to deal realistically with one's disability. A person may be required to admit that he is an alcoholic before being admitted to AA, not merely that he "has a drinking problem." Weight Watchers must admit that they are fat, not merely pleasingly plump. Acceptance of the harsh definition is used as an index of a commitment to change. Other groups have come to accept seemingly pejorative labels as a sign of full acceptance of one's status, including such terms as *dike* (Daughters of Bilitis), *dope fiend* (Synanon), *mad* (Mental Patients Liberation Front), and *convict* (Prisoners' Union). This tendency to *dysphemism* indicates less a desire to take the oppressor's definition of self than a declaration of kinship with other outcast people. Wearing a derogatory label as a badge of honor, as some police have done with the term *pig* (local police and sheriffs clash in a football game known as the Pig Bowl), also helps to dissipate the paleologic. Police who have played in the Pig Bowl will be less offended by the term than other policemen for whom it has been exclusively a term of derogation.

The opposite position to that of Orwell is that name-changing represents an idealistic non-solution to tangible problems. Rather than pettifogging about language, efforts should be directed to changing policies and instituting reforms. The compromise position between these two views is that clear and meaningful terminology is indispensable in planning and carrying out meaningful reforms, but cannot be an end in itself. The critical issue is whether there can be meaningful discussion with the old terms or whether it would be helpful to replace them. In the prison field, my vote goes for using the terms already there. Name-changing has such a bad record in this field that it has become synonymous with hypocrisy and tokenism. There are sufficient terms around to suit any purpose. I can see nothing to be gained in replacing *prison* or *inmate* with whatever happens to be the latest vogue term. *Jail* has a special meaning as a place of short-term confinement, where people await trial or serve short sentences. Such places are managed by local authorities rather than by state or federal agencies; thus in England they are called *locals*. *Jail* comes from a Latin word meaning *cage* or *den*. Another common term in England for a place of short-term confinement is *lock-up*. Willie Holder, the head of the Prisoners' Union, would like to see *inmate* replaced by its antecedent *convict* to reinforce the idea that the offender has been convicted of an offense. The origins of *inmate* are tied to institutions (in-mate), and this is discordant with the goal of keeping offenders in the community. However, *convict* goes back to the Latin *con* (wholly) and *vincere* (to conquer), suggesting that the convicted person has been wholly overcome (convinced) by the proof of his guilt. One could also return to *felon* (a wicked person), *misdemeanant* (one who has engaged in wrong behavior), or *offender* (to dash or thrust against), but all of these terms have obvious disadvantages. Either they require that one has been locked up or they emphasize lawbreaking, when in fact most people who break the law never see the inside of a prison cell. The solution, it seems, is to use in an appropriate context words about which a reasonable consensus of meaning exists. Also these terms should be employed in a straightforward, objective and non-pejorative manner. For the ensuing chapters we will use terms such as *inmate, convict, offender,* and *felon* interchangeably. If there are special nuances to the usage (e.g. felons, as distinct from misdemeanants), this will be apparent from the context. Declaring words taboo places an emotional aura about them. It also limits discussion to those people willing to adopt a particular usage.

Some of the attempts to change prison names are deliberately deceptive. The change from "the Hole" to "the Adjustment Center" in California prisons was a straightforward attempt at euphemism. However, the most recent change to "Security Housing Units" is more sinister. After a court decision that an inmate was entitled to a formal hearing before being transferred to a disciplinary unit, state authorities renamed the Adjustment Centers "Security Housing Units" (SHU, or "the Shoe" to inmates) and took the position that such transfers represented merely a change in housing assignment which would not require a judicial hearing. Occasionally there are some very practical and humane reasons behind efforts to rename institutions. Congress appropriated a large amount of money for hospital construction in 1946 under the Hill-Burton Act. It quickly became apparent that these monies could go to mental hospitals as well as general medical facilities. All across the nation there was a great rush to rename state homes, asylums, and training schools. Parson's Training School (for the retarded) in Kansas quickly became The Parson's State School and Hospital. The resultant ambiguity still plagues the state mental hygiene system in that it is now necessary to ask whether a state hospital is for MR or MI patients (mentally retarded or mentally ill). Although no one can blame the state officials who renamed their institutions to be eligible for sizable construction grants, it would have been preferable for Congress to have either included them in the first place or restricted the grants to general medical facilities if that was its intention.

State officials constantly complain about the problems of finding a location for new prisons; citizens who believe prisons are necessary still do not want one located nearby. In the hopes of gaining greater community acceptance, state officials have resorted to euphemism.

This approach is effective only until the neighbors find out the actual nature of the operation, and then they complain that they were deceived as well as imposed upon. The real problem is that a prison is an ugly place that corrupts everyone associated with it. When prisons are improved to the point where they no longer brutalize and debase, most of the problems of locating them in populated areas will disappear.

Euphemism and paleologic are intimately related. Euphemism is used to cover paleologic; and releasing the paleologic destroys the usefulness of the euphemism. Professional jargon is a meta-language designed to avoid the effects of paleologic. The psychiatrist prefers to talk of psychopaths, anti-social personalities, and character disorders, rather than rapists, robbers, and murderers. The danger in using this sort of meta-language is that the concepts become reified as the playthings of professions. People start thinking about psychopathy and character disorders as if they were real entities in the world rather than terms for classifying segments of behavior. Such terms will only describe a small fraction of a person's behavior. A "homosexual" may also be a Baptist, husband, accountant, and skydiver. The "embezzler" may have an unblemished record of community service until tempted in a moment of weakness. When such terms are represented to be global descriptions of personality, they distort more than they convey. Still, by blunting the emotional force of paleologic, both euphemism and the meta-language of the social sciences make it easier to discuss "hot" issues. In the best cases, however, social science terminology goes further than euphemism, in using meta-language as tongs to handle emotional material that could not otherwise be touched. But social science jargon fails insofar as it remains separate from action. There is an old adage in corrections that classification without differential treatment is meaningless.

We must drain away the paleologic from crime and punishment if we are to develop rational means of handling offenders. This will not be easy, but psychiatry, psychology, and the other social sciences have been developing tools to do it. The survey techniques of Alfred Kinsey have been criticized for depriving sexual behavior of its emotional content and seemingly reducing sex to frequency and type of outlet.[10] This criticism has some validity; but draining away the paleologic that is so prized by poets, playwrights, and priests is the necessary precursor to scientific discussion. Kinsey embarked on a pioneer study when he explored the sexual habits of all sorts of people, not merely a small group of deviants. Publication of his results helped to leach the paleologic from many sexual practices that previously could not be discussed in meaningful terms. Kinsey found that his respondents were willing to discuss some of the most intimate aspects of their sexual lives with a surprising degree of candor. At the conclusion of the sessions, many of those interviewed thanked Kinsey for providing them with the opportunity to discuss some of these topics openly for the first time in their lives.

A similar survey of the general population in the area of crime would have many beneficial effects. It would help drain away the mystique from crime and permit us to develop a terminology suited to all sorts of lawbreaking, not merely to a small category of losers. The classification system developed by the FBI may be appropriate for record-keeping, but this does not make it the best meta-language for understanding criminality. When researchers leave their offices and go out in the community and start asking about crime, both reported and unreported, their data have a refreshing significance that is ordinarily absent in crime statistics. They learn that most rapes and a sizable number of burglaries go unreported and that most victims of crime are black and brown. One can barely imagine the results of Kinsey-type depth interviews on such topics as income tax fraud, expense account cheating, embezzlement, illegal gambling, and prohibited sexual practices. A comprehensive view of lawbreaking would be very different from the ordinary tabulations of arrest rates, convictions, and imprisonment.

THE NEW VIOLENCE 4

When inmates come into San Quentin for the first time, the place just terrorizes them. The staff at San Quentin all ought to have presidential citations for running it as well as they do. RAYMOND PROCUNIER

There is very little precedent for the wave of individual stabbings and assaults plaguing American prisons today. There were occasional stabbings in old-line prisons, perhaps a half-dozen incidents a year, but there was nothing like San Quentin's record of 85 reported stabbings (in addition to unrecorded incidents) in 1974. The concern of the authors of *Prevention of Violence in Correctional Institutions,* published in 1973, is solely with riots and other collective disturbances.[1] Corrections texts written before 1970 gave little attention to individual assaults, which were viewed as the aberrations of deranged inmates or occasionally the results of feuds brought in off the streets. What distinguishes the new violence from the old is not only its greater frequency but its use of steel weaponry rather than fists.

It has been well documented that violence in prison comes in waves. The first incident usually means more is on the way. This includes violence directed towards the self, as expressed in mutilation and suicide. In Canada's Saint Vincent de Paul Penitentiary, during several months of 1972, an average of three inmates a day slashed themselves.[2] Prison riots, which have increased sharply in the past twenty-five years, are also contagious. Jackson, Michigan, in 1952 began a year of rioting which included more than 25 institutions. In 1955 another series of disturbances began in Walla Walla, Washington, and spread to institutions throughout the country. In 1969 there were 39 reported riots, and in 1970 this increased to 59. At no time in American history has there been a significant amount of violence by inmates directed towards staff. The death of a guard during a prison disturbance is an accident, a reprisal, or a by-product of the indiscriminate fighting that accompanies an attempt to suppress the disturbance. Inmates have not organized themselves deliberately to kill, wound, or even physically abuse their keepers, and the amount of violence directed by inmates towards one another exceeds by a thousandfold the documented incidents of violence directed by inmates towards guards. In practice even a single incidence of violence towards the guards will provoke the strongest counter-reaction from the authorities. A year-long lockdown of California prisons followed the death of a guard in an institution where dozens of inmates were injured in assaults every year. Typically there is a determined effort to play down violence among inmates. Statistics of inmates injured in assaults are difficult to locate. It is only when the situation reaches epidemic proportions, and begins to include staff or the outside community, that the authorities are compelled to act.

The situation at Alabama's two prisons is typical in this respect:

> The "normal" level of tension and violence at these two prisons suddenly escalated in mid-January, 1974, when some inmates at Atmore took two guards hostage, seized control of part of the prison and demanded negotiations and publicity about prison conditions. The warden quickly led an armed charge that ended the Atmore rebellion. Its toll was two dead and scores injured, almost all of them inmates. Partly because one of the dead men was a guard, this eruption touched

> off headlines and investigations and charges that ran on for weeks, until eclipsed in March by an outbreak at Holman which also cost the lives of a guard and a prisoner. The local grand jury sitting in the county seat of Brewton soon voted a long list of indictments against inmates on charges ranging from riot to first-degree murder of the guards who died in the two uprisings. No guards or officials were indicted for their roles in the violence or for the hideous prison conditions surrounding the two fatal incidents.[3]

The absence of reliable data on prison violence is a serious handicap to prison administrators. It is generally recognized that recorded incidents of assaults are only a fraction of all those that occur. The sanctions against "ratting" suppress all but the most flagrant incidents. Many of the inmates with the longest terms are there for offenses committed inside the prison. A single infraction or suspicion of a rule violation can add years to a man's sentence and an assault can make it a life term. Wesley Wells entered prison in 1928 for receiving stolen property. He eventually left forty-six years later. In between there were charges of manslaughter in 1931, possession of a knife in 1944, and assault on another prisoner in 1947. John B. Hill and Charles Pernasilice were in their teens and never should have been in Attica prison at the time of the 1971 rebellion. Both youths should have been in institutions for juvenile offenders, not a state prison for felons. Today Pernasilice faces one to four years and Hill a life sentence for assaulting and killing a prison guard. Prior to the indictment, the only criminal conviction of Pernasilice was for the theft of a motorcycle when he was sixteen.

There are many kinds of violence rampant in prison other than collective disturbances and knifings. Sexual assaults are a problem in every penal institution in the country, although the problem is more severe in jails than in prisons. The Davis Report on sexual assaults in Philadelphia jails conservatively estimated that during a 26-month period, there were approximately 2000 sexual assaults involving 1500 individual victims and 3500 individual aggressors.[4] In prisons the presence of inmate gangs serves as a deterrent to rape. Gangs will not tolerate the rape of a brother, and to assault someone from another gang would be provocative. Particularly for a young inmate, the fear of sexual assault is one of the chief inducements for joining a gang. However, this kind of protection system has many drawbacks, in terms of both repaying one's protectors with sexual favors and the frequent disputes between rival gangs. Sexual assaults are so common in jails that they are considered by authorities and inmates alike to be part of punishment. Criminal prosecution of the assailant is infrequent and unsuccessful. Complaints are discouraged by guards, and prisoners are frequently punished for merely complaining. They may be put into isolation "for their own protection," but the net effect is the same as in punitive segregation. Internal disciplinary hearings are not likely to be more successful. According to the ACLU, the most promising method for inmates who have been sexually assaulted is the civil lawsuit.[5] Until damage suits by inmates who have been sexually assaulted are successful, no progress can be made in reducing the number of such incidents.

Idealism

The first response of authorities to the wave of individual violence was to look for scapegoats. It is always easier to find someone to blame than to seriously examine the conditions that give rise to pathology. The tendency to reduce behavior to individual psychology has a long tradition in American philosophy under the name of idealism or psychological reductionism. What characterizes all such approaches is the assertion that human perceptions and motives are primary and situations secondary. Haney, Banks, and Zimbardo speak of this as the *dispositional hypothesis,* or the attempt to explain unwholesome prison conditions as due to the personalities of inmates (compulsive, aggressive, and psychopathic) and the kind of guards who work there (uneducated, unmotivated, and poorly paid).[6] Every philosophical doctrine carries within it the seeds of its own opposition; and the antithesis of idealism is realism, which maintains that objects and situations have an independent existence.* Idealism and realism suggest diametrically opposite reform strategies. When problems are reduced to the personalities and motives of the keepers and inmates, the obvious solution is to improve the people or replace them with better people. Responding to criticism of the state's prison system, former Georgia governor Lester Maddox declared, "We are doing the best we can. And before we can do much better, we are going to have to get a better grade of prisoner." [7] The environmentalist approach is to search for the specific conditions that constrain people to act as they do and then alter those conditions. Nowhere is this dichotomy of views more apparent than in the proposed solutions to prison violence. Psychological reductionism attributes violence to the personalities and motives of the people involved; realism/environmentalism sees violence as a coping mechanism in an institution whose existence rests upon the application of force.

Freudian psychiatry provides the theoretical props for psychological interpretations of prison violence. Prison officials issue press releases about a new kind of convict they describe as a "violence-prone psychopath." In today's pop psychiatry, this means someone who doesn't obey the rules. When told that one-third of prison inmates are psychopaths, the public finds it easy to accept violence as a natural condition of prison life. No one can argue with the proposition that violence comes from "violence-prone psychopaths," but this circular reasoning gets us nowhere. Trying to solve the problems of the prison according to idealistic precepts, authorities transfer or segregate difficult inmates. Large amounts of money are spent to construct maxi-maxi cellblocks separate from the mainline. The tension in these segregated areas rises to unbearable levels, without denying inmates the opportunity to injure

* There are obvious difficulties in using terms such as *idealism* and *realism,* whose technical philosophical meanings depart so greatly from popular usage. In common speech, the idealist is an incorrigible dreamer while the realist is practical and logical. These are not the connotations of the technical definitions. To reinforce the fact that the technical rather than the popular usage is intended here, I will combine the terms with others, e.g. realism/environmentalism or idealism/psychological reductionism.

one another. Oklahoma's prison-within-a-prison, the scene of frequent disturbances, is known as The Rock, named after Alcatraz. In San Quentin in 1974 most of the numerous stabbings took place in maximum-security areas where special lock-up procedures had been instituted. Some Texas prisons place inmates who are considered troublemakers into cells with known homosexuals as a form of punishment. Another way to remove troublemakers has been to transfer them frequently before they can establish a following in the yard. This puts a lot of people on the road at any single time and further destabilizes the inmate social order.

Fistfights between prisoners used to be regarded as safety valves for discharging tensions that might otherwise be directed at staff. The increasing use of lethal weaponry has changed this. Fights which used to end up with a beating escalate now into a widening spiral of stabbings and fatalities. However, there is still some support for the tension-reduction view of prison violence. When a prison is too quiet too long, guards feel uneasy. They have come to expect, and sometimes will provoke, periodic violence to release submerged tensions. Following the same logic, consensual homosexuality is tolerated as a means of reducing tensions on the tiers even though many officers realize that the sexual jealousies can produce serious altercations.

The threat of violence permeates every contact between inmate and guard. The guard represents an electrified wire which may at any time send the alarm to the central office and beyond. The guard knows that he carries this electrical charge within him. A bad guard abuses it by pushing an inmate to the limit, hoping to provoke him to some fateful response. The wary inmate knows the consequences of striking or speaking harshly, so he swallows his anger. It will emerge later in some casual contact between the man who was abused and his fellow inmates. Swallowing all this tension would in the outside world produce ulcers. Among inmates the tension emerges as assaults on one another and fantasies about the society that maintains this kind of system. George Jackson described how violence directed by a guard towards an inmate emerged later as violence between inmates:

> I have seen the "keeper" slap a man at the food serving line, take his tray, and send him back to his cell without dinner. The man that was slapped may have been old enough to be the keeper's father. The urge to strike out at the "keeper" will almost always be repressed. In fact, most of the spontaneous fist fights between inmates occur immediately following an encounter between one of the participants of the fight and a "keeper." [8]

Contrary to press reports of stabbings and riots, the outward attitude of inmates towards the staff is not hatred but the servility of a slave towards his master. Violence is inherent in the dominance/subordination relationship, first as the threat of force behind the keeper's orders and second as the inmate's submerged response to brutality. The lack of any legitimate channel for inmate grievances and the immediate consequences of expressing any direct criticism of the guards make violence between inmates inevitable. To anyone who thinks of convicts as hot-blooded and aggressive, the tight discipline of a maximum-security prison is a remarkable sight. Inmates learn quickly to submit to innumerable indignities in the name of security and order. Imagine being stripped and skin-searched by club-wielding guards several times a day, including occasional "finger wipes" (rectal inspections), with nothing to look forward to except several years of the same. Without romanticizing people who have broken the law, one can say that most inmates show a high degree of self-control. In any prison yard a common sight is inmates doing calisthenics, performing innumerable push-ups, lifting weights, punching bags, and otherwise keeping themselves in prime physical shape. Everyone looks as if he is in training, but in training for what? The idealistic explanation is that the inmates exercise constantly because they are physical creatures. While there are many mesomorphs (muscular types with a high need for physical activity) among inmates, the constant working out is a logical response to long periods of confinement as well as the need to keep one's self in shape to maintain a place in the inmate social order. A weak inmate unable to defend his rights is bound to be exploited unless he has powerful friends. In a very real sense, being in good physical shape is survival insurance.

A significant factor in the new violence is the presence of steel weaponry either smuggled in or manufactured in prison. One inmate described the coldest sound he ever heard as another inmate prying his bed back and forth in order to remove a steel slat from the wall which he then proceeded to sharpen throughout the rest of the night. Periodic inspections, shakedowns, and skin searches attempt to retrieve hidden weapons. The Hawaii State Prison was recently invaded by 200 National Guardsmen armed with M16 rifles, shotguns, and gas projectiles, wearing flack jackets, Plexiglas helmets, and battle fatigues. The guardsmen removed each inmate from his cell, gave him a skin search, and then checked each cell thoroughly. There was no riot at the time, and the total population of the prison consisted of only 200 inmates, yet the record of previous violence had led Hawaii's lieutenant governor to describe the situation as hopeless. This reveals the fallacy of believing that reducing the size of penal institutions will automatically improve things. It is true that the buildings and facilities of Hawaii State Prison were decrepit and, in the words of a state legislator who toured the facility, "unfit for human habitation." However, the Lucasville (Ohio) State Prison, while still so new that it had not been officially accepted by the state from the contractor, already had guards' strikes, inmate riots, various murders, and innumerable other difficulties in a building that cost $24 million.

Inmate Gangs

Even more popular as scapegoats for prison violence than psychopaths, permissive parents, lenient judges, interfering politicians, and bleeding-heart liberals are inmate gangs. These have always played an important part in the prison social system, but now prison officials see them as revolutionary violence-prone organizations. Today they are based largely on race, geography, and ideology. The groups seem remarkably stable despite the frequent transfer of identified gang members. Some are regional and others national, with names like the Black Guerrilla Family, the Black Liberation Front, the Young Lords, the Mexican Mafia, La Familia, and the Aryan Brotherhood. Violence in the prison is seen by prison officials as an outgrowth of a struggle between the various gangs for members and control of the lucrative drug trade. Racial aspects are particularly serious in New York and California prisons, where the presence of a third major ethnic group, Puerto Ricans in New York and Chicanos in California, contributes to the instability of the inmate social order. There are divergent views among penologists regarding cliques and gangs. The extreme view that any association among lawbreakers is bad produced the solitary confinement of the Quaker penitentiary and the silent system of the Auburn prison. The courts have also recognized the unique psychological pressures in the prison society: "The association between men in correction institutions is closer and more fraught with physical danger and psychological pressures than is almost any other kind of association between human beings." [9] Many officials believe that unrestricted association between convicts leads inevitably to gangs and cliques which brutalize weaker inmates, harass those who will not join, and pose a threat to the administration. This view was forcefully stated by New York State Corrections Commissioner Russell Oswald: "I would not tolerate gangs, cliques, and bullies. . . . I was determined to make it possible for men to serve out their sentences in peace." [10] Oswald saw the common denominator of all inmate groups as predatory, illegal activities. His solution was the quick transfer of gang leaders and troublemakers.

The mark of idealism/subjectivism in these explanations is the lack of any attempt to understand the conditions that impel inmates to join gangs or engage in assaults. The impression is created that gangs are fighting because they are fighting gangs; violence-prone psychopaths join forces to fight one another. However, in current psychiatric thinking, psychopaths are loners and make very poor gang members. They are far too unpredictable and impulsive to maintain firm discipline or loyalty. Like all idealistic explanations, the conclusion that inmates are violent, amoral, and impulsive because they are psychopaths is inherently circular. It would be equally legitimate to conclude that inmates are psychopaths because they are violent, amoral, and impulsive. We do not attribute the high frequency of homosexuality in prisons to the "kind of inmate" behind bars. Rather, we attribute it to sexual deprivation in a society of one sex. We could make a similar interpretation of the extensive violence that goes on behind bars. Rather than seeing it as a product of this kind of inmate, it can be related to the social, economic, and political pressures of imprisonment. Racial strife in prison is hardly surprising in view of the centuries of discrimination and segregation against minority inmates. The most common reason inmates give for joining gangs is survival. Subsidiary reasons include a piece of the action in terms of good housing assignments, soft jobs, and drugs and other contraband items. Black, brown, and other minority inmates found they had to organize in order to receive their share of decent jobs and even seats near the television set.

In the outside world there are numerous ways by which humans have reduced violence among themselves. Territoriality keeps potentially warring factions out of each other's way. So long as people know where they belong spatially they are not likely to get into trouble. An accepted social order is another way of minimizing conflicts. People who know where they stand socially don't have to spend a great deal of time testing out their rank. Formal treaties, compacts, and agreements are another means by which conflicts are avoided. These methods are difficult to apply in the microcosm of the prison. Space is so limited that it is not possible to mark out and defend territories. There will be temporary jurisdictions over certain areas, but the large number of people and the limited amount of space virtually guarantee spillover and conflict. The social order is always in flux with the addition of new men and attrition through discharge or transfer. A key factor in destabilizing the social order is the hostility of prison authorities to inmate gangs and the transfer of gang leaders. The lack of recognized leaders, and absence of turf, and the illegitimacy of the inmate's bargaining position make it difficult to develop and enforce compacts, agreements, or treaties. This leaves individual violence as the remaining means of settling disputes. It is fairly obvious that the authorities are neither willing nor able to settle disputes within the inmate society. Given the number of people behind bars because of their quick tempers and inability to restrain impulses, the occasional flare-up in prison is understandable. Once an assault, stabbing, or killing takes place, the lack of internal restraining mechanisms is likely to produce an escalating cycle of violence.

Such a situation was responsible for the recent rise of homicides among Philadelphia street gangs; over forty black youths died in gang fights in 1974. To understand the sources of violence, J. B. Lieber, a young white law student, spent time running with the street gangs.[11] He attributed the rise of homicides to the police policy of destroying the ghetto social order. Until the 1960s, Philadelphia averaged about three gang deaths a year. There were many gang fights or rumbles, but these were highly organized activities, led by warlords, with judges, diplomats, and "check holders" who made treaties and organized "fair ones"—weaponless fights to settle disputes over turf. At some point, police mounted a determined campaign to arrest gang leaders. According to Lieber, "It would be impossible for a young man to be a gang leader today, for all the police attention he would receive." Treaties, diplomats, and fair fights have been replaced by guerrilla-style individual violence. A jitterbug from one gang will surreptitiously enter another gang's turf to avenge a wrong. Operating solo, he is forced to rely on lethal weapons. Gang members don't like this new style of doing things. Most would prefer the old method of treaties, rumbles, and fair fights, but they feel helpless to reverse the escalated violence. With the arrest and harassment of gang leaders, all the hierarchies have broken down, and, according to Lieber, enough gang leaders have been jailed to organize a turf-by-turf microcosm of the city in all the local detention facilities. Ironically, time in the slammer is one of the prime requisites for being a leader on the streets, producing a kind of a revolving door back into the prison system.

Racism

Discussion of inmate gangs is impossible without mentioning racism. Race is the chief defining characteristic in prison life, superseding all distinctions except the one between guard and inmate, and sometimes that. Racism is the assumption of inherent racial superiority or any program of racial domination based on such an assumption. The American prison with its white guards and colored inmates fits this definition. Attica in 1971, with its 70 per cent black and brown inmates and 100 per cent white staff, is an extreme instance of an endemic situation. Since 1971 the number of black and Puerto Rican correctional officers in New York State has been doubled, but they still account for fewer than 15 per cent of correctional staff, while the inmate population remains 75 per cent black and Puerto Rican. Everywhere in the country it is the lowest economic stratum that is most heavily represented in prison. In South Dakota it is the Native Americans who are over-represented behind bars, in the Southwest it is the Chicanos, and in New York it is the blacks and Puerto Ricans. The low percentage of Asian-Americans behind bars indicates that it is not color itself that makes the difference but membership in an economically and socially deprived minority. The pattern of de facto discrimination pervades every aspect of the criminal justice system, from arrest to plea-bargained sentences, time served, and parole conditions.

William Nagel has documented how blacks in the federal prison system receive longer sentences than their white counterparts.[12] Matched for number of previous offenses, blacks average 5 additional months for assault, 19 additional months for drugs, 6 for embezzlement, 5 for robbery, and so on. The federal prison system is, according to Nagel, becoming blacker and blacker. So too are the local jails and state prisons. In the Philadelphia County Jail, 95 per cent of the inmates are black; Pennsylvania, which has an overall black population of 9.4 per cent, has a local jail population of 62.9 per cent black. The Illinois Statesville Penitentiary, a 2000-man maximum-security institution thirty miles from Chicago, is 70 per cent black, 10 per cent Latin, and 20 per cent white. To survive, inmates join gangs based upon ethnic affiliation, and these gangs run the prison. Studies by the American Association of University Women determined that bails and fines tended to be higher and sentences longer for black women than for white women on similar charges.[13] Describing the Muncie, Indiana, jail, Kitsi Burkhart wrote, "Like many jails for women, Muncie has no black staff. Though 40% of the prisoners are black, and even more from urban areas, the staff is rural and white, largely middle aged housewives who had no professional background or training." [14]

Even the news reporting of crimes and arrests shows a racial bias. The Community Renewal Society made a study of homicide in Chicago in 1973 and compared actual police records with crime reports in the *Chicago Tribune,* the major newspaper in the city. They found that 51 of the 215 murders in the city during 1973 were covered by the *Tribune* and 12 were mentioned in stories that ran on the first 5 pages. While only 20 per cent of the murder victims during this period were white, and 80 per cent were black or other minority people, nearly half of the 51 murder stories concerned white victims. On the first 5 pages, where reader interest is highest, two-thirds of the murder stories involved white victims.[15]

Ironically, some government bureaus have been loath to publicize figures on the over-representation of minority people in jail for fear of being labeled racist. Concealment of the high proportion of minority inmates, and their longer sentences and higher rate of disciplinary infractions, will only perpetuate the racism and class bias of the criminal justice system. Racial segregation remains the prevalent pattern in the American prison although it is largely de facto rather than de jure—i.e. a fact of prison life rather than required by law. U.S. District Judge Luther Bohanon found the Oklahoma State Department of

Corrections guilty of racial segregation in housing, recreational activities, dining-hall seating, and inmate job assignments, and of imposing disciplinary penalties more often and more severely on black inmates than on white inmates guilty of comparable rule violations. Prison authorities justify this segregation as a means of reducing violence.

That this situation has been of long duration is apparent from examining records of American prisoners 100 years ago. The history of the North Carolina prison system was extensively researched by Jesse Steiner and Roy Brown.[16] Prior to the Civil War, there were relatively few prisoners in North Carolina, and no state prison existed; in 1848 the citizens of North Carolina had specifically voted against establishing a state prison. Slaves who broke the law were dealt with by their own masters. However, the situation changed completely after the Civil War, when local and county jails began to overflow with freed slaves. Suddenly there was a tangible need for a state prison. According to Steiner and Brown, ''Within two decades following the Civil War the problem of the southern prison, state and county, became pre-eminently the problem of dealing with the negro prisoner.''

Guards and administrators sometimes use racial animosity as a management tool. Years ago control was achieved by administration support of the prerogatives of the con bosses who maintained internal order. The decline of the old-style criminal gang and the rise of the ideological and racial gang have led to a new tactic in which the administration tries to maintain control by manipulating racial animosities. One group is told that the other group is out to get them. Black inmates complain that the guards will give weapons to white inmates and intervene only when a white inmate is getting the worst of the struggle. ''A fist fight, a temporary, trivial loss of control will bring a fusillade of bullets down upon the darker of the two men fighting,'' declared George Jackson.[17] The white guard feels great anxiety about being isolated in a yard among so many black and brown faces. This is something new and frightening to a poorly educated white guard from a predominantly rural white area. Nor do I envy the situation of a recently hired black prison psychologist going out into those sections of the yard controlled by the white inmates. The tension of the San Quentin yard is so intolerable that inmates request to be locked up after lunch rather than mingle and risk assault or worse. Everyone in prison knows the significance of guards putting a black inmate in a tier controlled by whites, or a white inmate in an area controlled by blacks. In prison vernacular, the inmate is being "set up." There is too much hatred and tension, too long a history of racial antagonism for short-term accommodations to evolve, no chance for reasoned discussion or dialogue, just to fight it out. Many of the most notable inmates have served most of their time for crimes committed while behind bars. There is no way of knowing whether or not these men would have committed similar crimes outside, but there seems a distinct causal connection between the racism, sexual deprivation, alienation, and crowding of the prison and the violence it spawns.

Outside Agitators

Blaming one's critic is a familiar response to failure. In the prison system the critics are described as "outside agitators" or "an unsympathetic press." Commenting on the suicide of eight guards in federal prisons in Quebec in 1973, the Canadian solicitor general declared that the guards were "too sensitive" to criticisms aimed at the penitentiary service and took them "too personally." [18] In the United States some officials blame prison unrest and violence on outside agitators—radical lawyers, Prison Rights groups composed largely of ex-cons, and liberal do-gooders who tell the inmate that the fault lies not within him but within society, that he is being unjustly held as a political prisoner, and that the main reasons for his being incarcerated are his race and class. Officials see this as a deliberate attempt to undermine the legitimacy of imprisonment. The myth has been developed that in the old days inmates at least accepted the fact that they had broken the law and were being punished. However, variations of today's radical critique were frequently heard within the prison of a century ago. There was a constant refrain that the big bosses and the white-collar criminals rarely got caught or went to prison if they slipped up, since the criminal justice system was full of crooked police, shyster lawyers, corrupt judges, and greedy politicians who took a percentage of everything. The legitimacy of imprisonment was no more accepted by inmates 100 years ago than it is today; the chief difference is that ethnic affiliation has moved to the forefront of consciousness. This is part of the cultural ethos rather than the work of a few radical lawyers.

Operating on the outside agitator theory, prison officials have tried to screen visitors and periodicals coming into prison. While some courts have taken a strong stand against censorship of inmate mail and visitors, these restrictive policies remain in effect. The involvement of inmates in the Symbionese Liberation Army (SLA), a terrorist group that came into prominence in the 1970s, was blamed by the California state corrections chief on the radicals who came into the prisons as part of a community relations program:

> These guys were coming in and intellectualizing with the inmates. . . . Here's a marine, here's a college professor, here's a beautiful woman coming in playing the sex role—pretty soon the inmates are part of it and they don't even know what they're part of.[19]

To speak of corruption by the young people involved in visiting programs seems particularly curious when one considers the usual history of the prisoner. Apart from the question of who is corrupting whom (most middle-class parents would be appalled at the thought of their college-age child, particularly a daughter, coming into contact with hardened criminals), the prisoner is perceived as some kind of half-witted dupe. Donald DeFreeze, otherwise known as General Field Marshal Cinque of the SLA, was described by a prison official as "a good, average, solid inmate . . . a very unsophisticated convict."[20] Considering persons as dupes implies that they are unable to develop ideas on their own and is a convenient means of dismissing their views. The most curious aspect of this theory is how these cons who have resisted the most powerful behavior change institutions of the society all their lives are suddenly brainwashed by a handful of young people in a few hours' time. Most cons have a long history of contact with school officials, probation officers, counselors, psychologists, and social workers, all of whom have been trained in the arts of attitude change. To suggest that prisoners who have effectively resisted the exhortations and authority of social workers, priests, and shrinks have suddenly crumbled and been brainwashed by a few hippie longhairs seems absurd. Clearly the model used is not one of attitude change but of contagion. The prisoners are seen as having "caught" the radical germ from their visitors, as a person might unsuspectingly and unresistingly catch chicken pox or measles. However, once DeFreeze escaped from prison, the brainwashing proceeded in the opposite direction. He was then described as controlling the other members of the group, particularly the women.

The most immediate result of the contagion theory is the reduction and elimination of promising programs for bringing more community people into penal institutions to provide a value system different from that of the inmate culture. There have also been attempts, based on the contagion theory, to screen attorneys and limit their visits. An anonymous inmate, testifying at a closed-door hearing of the California State Subcommittee on Civil Disorder, cited the radicalizing effect of prison visits on attorneys—"If they won't pack hacksaw blades for a man today, within a year they will, because they are just like prisoners. Their dedication grows as times goes by, too." [21]

The contagion model does have a germ of truth in it. The young people from Berkeley who visited Vacaville prison were profoundly moved by what they saw. Judges in Great Britain are encouraged to spend one or two days inside the jails to which they sentence people. And comments of twenty-three American judges who volunteered to spend one night in the Nevada State Prison ranged from "Appalling" to "Am I glad to get out of there, I didn't get five minutes sleep." A few of the judges spent the night in solitary confinement, including Judge Irwin Cantor of Phoenix, who unknowingly had a knife planted on him by the prison staff. Judge John Fitzgerald of Le Center, Minnesota, was shocked by the rampant homosexuality at the prison: "I wasn't kidding when I said I had to sleep on my back." [22]

No person can witness the dehumanizing irrationality of the American prison system and come away unchanged. This, more than security, is the main reason prison visitation programs have been so limited in scope and influence. The original conception of the penitentiary recognized the corrupting influence of the inmates on one another. However, the Philadelphia Quakers were not opposed to outside visitors coming to teach prisoners skills and help maintain links with the outside ("the visits of the virtuous cannot injure"). This at least was a rational model of contagion. The *National Observer* (June 15, 1974) carried interviews with four prominent ex-inmates of very different political persuasions—Jimmy Hoffa, Mickey Cohen, Philip Berrigan, and Dick Gregory. Each one described the crowding, dreariness, arbitrary rules, brutality, lack of job training, sexual deprivation, and the entire litany of complaints made by most every ex-prisoner. There was not a single hint by any of the interviewees that these problems were caused or compounded by outside agitators.

Numerous studies have revelaed the inability of experts to predict violent acts. When their views are taken seriously by the courts, psychiatrists tend to err on the conservative side in keeping people institutionalized longer than required. In 1966 the Supreme Court ruled, in *Baxtrom* v. *Herold,* that an offender could not be held in an institution for the criminally insane for a period longer than he would have served in prison for the same offense without proper judicial review. This decision resulted in the immediate transfer of 967 patients from New York's hospital for the criminally insane to regular civil hospitals. These patients were all alleged to have committed dangerous crimes, or were considered dangerous on the ward, and presumably would be a danger to the community too. Steadman and Cocozza followed these 967 men for four years after their transfer.[23] Only 26 caused trouble sufficient to require their return to a hospital for the criminally insane. Of the 98 who were released, 20 were arrested and 11 convicted, but only 2 of the offenses could be considered dangerous, and these were a single robbery and an assault. The low number of convictions among the released inmates seems significant in view of the likelihood that many would have remained indefinitely in hospitals for the criminally insane if this court decision had not been made. These 967 inmates had been institutionalized for an average of 15 years prior to the court decision. In 1968 McGrath published the results of his study of 293 murderers who were released from Broadmoor Hospital in England.[24] Not a single one had killed again. Steadman and Cocozza contacted McGrath four years after the publication of his study, and by this time only 1 of the 293 released murderers had killed someone. Psychiatrist John M. MacDonald undertook a follow-up study of 100 patients who had been hospitalized because they had made homicidal threats.[25] Six months after their release, only one had committed a deliberate murder to fulfill his threat. Surely these single murders are significant, as are the two violent offenses committed by the 98 released New York inmates; but our notion of civil liberties does not call for incarcerating a hundred people because a few might commit violent acts. Most psychiatrists will acknowledge their inability to predict violent behavior even on the part of their own patients. That they could make this kind of prediction in the case of people referred by the courts and seen under conditions of minimal rapport seems even more improbable. This kind of prediction requires knowledge of the *situations* in which people find themselves. Thus psychologists, psychiatrists, and sociologists spend more time analyzing and explaining riots and other forms of individual or group violence after they have occurred than in predicting them beforehand.

Seeking the historical antecedents of existing policies is a constructive activity. Looking for someone to blame and vilify is not. It is an historical fact that the Quakers were responsible for the first implementation in the United States of punishment through incarceration. The motives of the Quakers were humane, and their experiment attracted worldwide attention. There is little to be gained today in castigating colonial Americans for the evils in the present system, especially since Quakers are today in the vanguard of the prison reform movement. The American Friends Service Committee in 1975 proposed a two-year moratorium on prison construction, directed specifically at the plans of the Federal Bureau of Prisons to build between forty-five and sixty-six new prisons by 1981.

Blame, like long-term incarceration, is an ineffective punishment—it doesn't deter, reform, or re-educate. Blame makes people defensive and resentful, it hinders rather than helps reasoned discussion. It diverts attention from environmental conditions and places it on individuals and groups, many of whom have long since departed. A more productive approach than seeking scapegoats is to understand the actions of individuals within the social, historical, and institutional framework in which they find themselves. Behavior does not reside within individuals in terms of fixed traits, but rather in dispositions to act in particular ways depending upon the situation. Walter Coutu called these *tinsits* or tendencies-in-situation.[26] Given the right situation, the individual will act in a predictable way. If you can stipulate the situations in which people will find themselves and know something about their tinsits, you can accurately predict their behavior. Otherwise, knowing only personality traits and nothing about situations, one deals in prophecy. This is why social scientists so rarely try to predict behavior and instead concentrate their efforts on explaining what has taken place in the past, and why those attempts to predict actual behavior—such as a propensity to violence—have yielded negative results.

Roles, while influential, do not completely determine behavior. Some prison guards are particularly brutal, while others remain only spectators to brutality; and, incidentally, it seems difficult to predict these differences from any sort of personality tests. However, such differences in degree are overwhelmed by the mutual antagonisms and fear that pervade all aspects of prison life. Joining an inmate gang is not a sign of neurosis in any psychiatric sense. It is more logically viewed as a constructive attempt to redress a power imbalance. The slogan of prison authorities—do your own time—is a prescription for a schizoid adaptation. The good inmate, according to the staff definition, minds his own business, shows no emotion, and keeps his opinions to himself; to the old-style guard, there is no such thing as constructive activity among inmates. This is not an unrealistic perception in an institution dominated by criminal values. With the exception of those inmates who have graduated through a series of juvenile institutions and find security in the prison environment, every single inmate and staff member has his character warped by the prison experience. This is also true for those inmates and guards who are able to detach themselves emotionally from what is going on around them, and perform their daily activities as zombies. Prison violence is not basically a product of personal pathology, although this may contribute to it. The same personal pathology under other circumstances does not produce this sort of violence. Rather the violence is inherent in an institution which assembles large groups of lawbreakers in one place, prevents contact with the outside world, and denies them a legitimate bargaining position.

LOSERS KEEPERS 5

Prison work is thankless. The public has no idea when a prison is well run; the only appreciation comes from the few prison authorities who know what a peculiar art this is. You live continually on the edge of disaster. WARDEN F. S. BALDI

The failure of the prison system has produced a pervasive atmosphere of discouragement, distrust, and defensiveness. Nobody trusts anyone. Each person sees himself as trapped in a system he cannot control. There is a daily flow of cases from the streets to the institutions that seems inexorable. The policeman on the beat can at some point regulate the flow, but he is frustrated by his inability to remedy the conditions leading people to crime. Judges seem all-powerful on the bench, but in private admit their inability to affect the events they are supposed to control. The individual judge is "caught in the inexorable day-to-day grinding out of the endless opening and closing of cases in a drama where none of the actors has much control over how the play is managed." [1]

Corrections staff express resentment towards the courts who supply them with clients and impose discriminatory sentences that make their work more difficult. They believe that the police, district attorneys, and judges, who are more highly paid and esteemed, look down upon them as second-rate professionals. With their B.A.'s in sociology and psychology, professional corrections staff constitute a liberal establishment within the criminal justice system. At any law enforcement conference it is they who express the most liberal positions on any controversial issue, e.g. revising the marijuana laws or capital punishment. Perhaps it is always the fate of a liberal establishment to be caught between conflicting pressures from the right and left. Identified as part of a punitive system by those on the left and as ineffectual do-gooders by those on the right, rchabilitation counselors and probation officers are frustrated and isolated. The polarization of attitudes in the community deprives them of a constituency that would support and defend small-scale improvements. Trained corrections people proudly distinguish between their own education and background and that of colleagues who came up the ranks as police, prosecutors, or in the army. It is still the case that the majority of people in prison work, particularly at the top and bottom ends of the salary scale, are not trained specifically for the work. Programs in criminology, where they exist at all, tend to be stepchildren of the university.

Guards and other lower-echelon employees feel that they are not properly understood or supported by their superiors. Unable to rely on those above them, guards will make their own accommodations on the tiers independent of departmental policies, in order to insure their own safety.* These attitudes are most apparent in maximum-security institutions, which have "an atmosphere in which everyone seems more bored, more callous, more rigid—and more afraid." [2]

Although the data are somewhat sketchy, Thomas reports clinical evidence for personal adjustment problems among correctional officers

* A psychological analysis of the predicament of the guard or inmate cannot adequately portray the range or nuances of attitudes that exist. The adaptations of guards and inmates described here are typical rather than universal responses. Among both groups is represented a wide variety of attitudes and ideologies.

who have spent time in maximum-security settings.[3] Another study shows a higher incidence of coronary heart disease among line correctional officers than any other group of California state employees.[4] The most sensitive account of the effect of imprisonment upon the keepers comes not from a guard or a prison psychologist, but from an inmate, George Jackson. Sentenced for from one year to life for robbing a gas station, Jackson was in prison for more than ten years before his death in an escape attempt. "Any man," Jackson wrote, "who enters prison work with his feelings, his sensibilities, intact, must lose them or lose his job. . . . The days and months that a guard has to spend on the ground are what destroy anything at all that was good, healthy, or social about him before. Fear begets fear. And we come out with two groups of schizoids, one guarding the other." [5] Jackson identifies the pathology of the keepers as primarily a product of the impossible situation of keeping masses of men submerged for long periods.

On visits to prisons I have been impressed by the courteous and thoughtful attitude of the staff. From what I have seen, the standards for correctional officers in California are somewhat higher than in other states. However, even in California, virtually all of the guards' time is occupied in custodial duties—locking and unlocking doors, escorting inmates to the showers, the visiting area, to the dining hall, carrying out skin searches and stripping cells to find contraband, conducting body counts in the morning and afternoon, and pacing the catwalk, rifle in hand, ever vigilant for any departure from routine. This is not a role conducive to mental health. I am continually amazed that correctional officers bear up as well as they do. Prison reform will bring almost as much benefit to the correctional staff as it will to prisoners.

There is more to the guards' predicament than doing a dirty and difficult job. There is the terrible feeling that one's best efforts are wasted. For a similar kind of feeling we can look at the morale of soldiers fighting a lost cause. Stephen Smith, who volunteered for transfer to Vietnam because he was bored with his army duties in Germany, provides a devastating commentary on the lives of people whose daily work was rendered meaningless by larger events.[6] Small successes of army personnel were quickly negated. Territory occupied at great cost one day was abandoned the next. There was no end in sight and no rationality to the suffering. The soldier saw his friends being shot, equipment lost, all with no payoff, no sense of accomplishment, no underlying sense of purpose. Morale became lower and lower,and eventually everyone wanted out. The GI began to hate everyone, including the people he was supposedly fighting for, producing an attitude that "gooks aren't worth dying for." The result in many cases was extreme brutality and racism that did not end with the soldier's return home. There were no parades for returned soldiers, no public recognition that the job was worth doing, and people did not want to hear what the returned GI's had to say.

Like the returned veteran, the prison guard has little opportunity to discuss his experiences with a sympathetic audience. Most people do not want to hear about what goes on behind prison walls. They are interested in the activities of notorious inmates such as Lucky Luciano and Charles Manson; the publicity accorded the Watergate inmates briefly satisfied the celebrity mania of the American public. But when a guard tries to describe what it's like to be on the graveyard shift in a prison built in 1890, nobody wants to listen. Nor is he going to be regarded as a hero. Often the opposite is true. Thus his anger is directed at the prison reformer who seems to label him as a villain and the criminal as a victim. But the miasma of failure surrounding the prison destroys the guard's effectiveness in his relations with the inmate population. Any attempt at fraternization is regarded with suspicion by his fellow guards and with distrust by inmates. Prison employees feel that their problems are unique, nobody understands them, that the only people they can count on are their colleagues in the prison business, and even they may be unreliable. The feelings of waste and futility in prison work produce the blame syndrome discussed earlier. Occasionally the frustration comes out in brutality directed towards those individuals most accessible.

New York Commissioner Oswald asks what parents would think if their young son told them he wanted to be a prison guard when he grew up.[7] The question could be extended to include a prison psychologist, prison purchasing agent, prison cook, or a prison anything. Frederick Baldi, a prison physician who later became warden, describes his welcome into prison work by the senior physician: "Well you are now a prison physician—go bag your head. I hate to see a young man get into this lousy, low-down work." [8] The failure of imprisonment has undermined the legitimacy of everybody connected with it. Ex-convicts are stigmatized legally and morally, outsiders are regarded as naive and impractical, and insiders (cons, guards, and wardens) as biased. This has produced an anti-expert attitude that lends an unwarranted credibility to people untainted by the system. When it comes time to investigate prisons there is a determined effort to find people who have never been associated with the penal system.

The same distrust prevails even within those groups working for change. There is no single organization that represents the millions of Americans who have spent time behind bars. The stigma against acknowledging oneself an ex-con is the chief impediment to organizing inmates. There is an ideological and tactical schism between prison reformers (academics) and prison organizers (ex-cons). Some want to reform the system slowly through minor adjustments, others advocate a major overhaul, and still others want to scrap the old machine totally. There is the familiar split between experts by training, with official credentials and a power base in the system, and experts by experience who lack credentials and power. Among people subject to oppression, there is a belief that it takes one to help one—only a ——— can help another ———. (Fill in: alcoholic, drug addict, homosexual, or ex-convict). Rightly or wrongly, many inmates have concluded that prison reform benefits only the reformers. The militant prisoner organizations emphasize the financial stake that officials have in keeping prisons full. This model of economic motivation leaves no room for the outside reformer except as someone who wants to make money off the prison movement through articles, lectures, and lucrative consulting.

There is considerable precedent for this distrust of outsiders among the oppressed; a long period of reliance upon outside experts stifles indigenous leadership. This has given rise to proposals to increase the role of ex-convicts in the prison system.

Such suggestions imply that the wrong sorts of people have been attracted to the prison field and that many of the problems of imprisonment could be solved by hiring "the right people." With rare exceptions, proposals to hire ex-convicts in prison work have been strongly resisted by corrections staff, who see this as a further eroding of their own limited authority and status. There is every indication that most corrections people were originally men and women of humane outlook who became frustrated, alienated, and distrustful because they were trapped in an impossible system; Flynn admits that a person who is cynical or despairing cannot be expected to work honestly and effectively within the system.[9] This creates a real dilemma in finding and promoting the right personnel. While one does not want total cynics and pessimists, one would be equally well-advised to avoid Pollyannas who fail to perceive obvious defects. The only way a decent, intelligent person can remain within the prison system is to consciously work for change. I would not underestimate the difficulties of being part of the system that one is trying to change, but in corrections that is the only approach that can protect the employee against cynicism, despair, and self-recrimination.

There is no basis for believing that turning control of prisons over to inmates would make them any better places. Fortunately, this statement rests on more than conjecture. There is one state in the union where the convicts control the prisons. That state is Arkansas, where the inmates carry guns and the staff do not. State troopers who enter a prison must immediately surrender their guns to the inmate trustees, who return them later when the troopers leave. The inmates maintain the communication system between buildings, keep financial books and records, and do everything else that has to be done. This approach has been supported by successive governors, legislators, and the public on economic grounds. It is cheaper to let the inmates guard one another than to hire free-world people. The deplorable results of this policy were documented by Tom Murton, the former superintendent of the Tucker Prison.[10] Murton saw inmates who had been convicted of murder offenses in the gun turrets, fully armed. Strong inmates brutalized weaker inmates; they ran a flourishing drug trade and exploited others sexually. It was a society even more corrupt and brutal than those prevailing in institutions nominally controlled by guards.

Prisoners should have a voice in policies and procedures that affect them, but to turn the total control of an institution over to people who have shown an inability to obey the law and a propensity for violence virtually guarantees a violent, brutal, and corrupt society. On the other hand, increasing the power of correctional officials has not worked either. To give them greater control over the length of sentences would virtually guarantee that institutional adjustment would be the main criterion of a readiness for discharge.

Given the present racial composition of prisons, the white prison reformer is automatically subject to the accusation that he or she is a "nigger lover." This epithet implies that the reformer is necessarily acting against his or her own class interests by favoring the perpetrators of crime rather than the victims. It raises the issue of whether a reformer can be in good faith while acting against his or her own class interests. There is no easy answer to this charge, which has been leveled against several centuries of prison reformers. One can point out that street crime in the ghetto has bankrupted and driven out white merchants who owned grocery stores and liquor stores and lowered property values of buildings owned by whites. If one has reached the conclusion that society's use of imprisonment has caused more problems than it has solved and is both ineffective and expensive, then a more rational policy is in the interests of all segments of society, not merely those who are imprisoned. There may be some glamorous people somewhere for whom prison reform is a fashionable kick, although I personally do not move in those circles, but most of those people I have met working to improve prison conditions are serious and dedicated men and women. There are no careers or large sums of money to be made in prison reform. Investigative reporters and others such as

John Bartlow Martin, Jessica Mitford, and Ramsay Clark, who are identified with hard-hitting prison books, established their reputations long before venturing into the prison field. This is an area where, apart from a very few hardware suppliers and architects, there are no winners, even among the ranks of reformers.

Who Is Responsible?

While it is true that the flow of inmates to institutions is determined by the courts, following the mandates of the legislature and the enforcement practices of the executive branch, in practice all these systems are interconnected. Prison officials are complicit in the laws that send people to prison and keep them there for unnecessarily long periods. A well-documented aspect of the American political system is that groups and organizations control the boards intended to regulate them. The Department of Corrections in my state, as in many others, has full-time lobbyists working with the legislature and the Governor's Office and a public relations staff to influence the media. Even the Correctional Officers Association has a full-time paid lobbyist. The notion that corrections officials play no part in shaping the policies that affect them is totally false. Given the large amounts of money and jobs they control, corrections departments will exert considerable influence over the laws and policies supposedly "coming down" from the legislature or the executive branch. Like all other agencies in a complex society, corrections is affected by outside forces, although perhaps less than any single other government department. It could lobby for the reform of criminal statutes regarding drug use, homosexuality, and prostitution, but it doesn't. Revision of morals laws would remove prostitutes from women's jails and end the absurdity of arresting men for homosexual offenses and then sending them to institutions where homosexuality flourishes. Prison people must have a wider purview than the continuation of obsolete institutions. In a situation as complex and intertwined with everything else as corrections, the public is ultimately responsible, but the people most directly involved are those working professionally in the field. They are not the helpless pawns of a political chess match. Maybe they are not the kings and queens, but they control the castles, knights, and pawns, and I am really not sure about the bishops. They demean themselves and persuade nobody when they protest that they are merely the servants of the people. Jailers of the people, yes—servants, no. The vast amounts of money and the number of jobs involved, and the possibility of preying on the public fears of crime, have made prison managers a potent political force in state government. I look forward to the day when this entrenched political power is used to further meaningful change rather than to perpetuate an unworkable system.

The Failure Ethic

To understand how the prison system can continue to do such a poor job over such a long period of time, it is necessary to examine the American notion of accountability. There is an interesting double standard in our treatment of individuals and of institutions. If a young boy fails in school, he is stigmatized as hyperactive, retarded, or as an exceptional child, and placed in a special class where manual trades rather than academic skills are emphasized. We hire counselors to exhort and uplift those who have fallen and create special programs to help them return to society, but these special programs seem to lead only to other special programs. Our treatment of offenders follows this view of human accountability. The law regards the individual adult, unless he can prove some significant degree of mental incapacity from drugs or insanity, as responsible and accountable for his failure.

A very different notion of accountability is used when institutions fail. For over a century we have been incarcerating alcoholics in city jails at great expense and with no success whatever. No one pretends that this experience is beneficial except in the most minimal sense of providing shelter and food in the nightmare world of the drunk tank. Rather than discuss other ways of handling alcoholics—and a number of cities are finally developing programs outside the criminal justice system—I want to emphasize the notion of accountability employed in this situation. We do *not* hold the jails accountable for their failure to reform alcoholics. We don't even seriously question our laws and policies towards alcohol consumption. Instead we hold the alcoholic responsible for his condition and jail him for public drunkenness or disorderly conduct. The same conception of accountability is used when schools fail to teach students to read or add. The fault is with the students—their lack of motivation, their disinterest with traditional academic skills, their hyperactivity—or it may not be the child himself who is directly responsible for his failure, but rather his family and neighborhood, his malnutrition resulting from his parents' chronic unemployment, and the lack of intellectual stimulation during his formative years. No matter how sophisticated these explanations, their chief purpose is to shift responsibility for failure away from institutions onto individuals, families, and neighborhoods.

Society does everything it can to prop up the school system no matter how badly it works. We do not let institutions go bankrupt when they fail year after year, decade after decade. We have become so dependent on them that we cannot envisage bankruptcy. Too much money, too much real estate, and too many jobs are at stake in the continuation of the school system. Every effort to close unneeded schools or reduce teaching staffs to reflect declining enrollments has been strongly resisted by teachers and parents. Canada, like the United States, found itself with a surplus of expensive hospital beds at the end of the baby boom of the sixties. Presently, hospital costs account for more than half the budget of the Canadian National Health Plan even though only a small fraction of the number of patients treated are in hospitals. Despite these facts, there have been public demonstrations and protest marches to protest the closing of hospitals. Political liabilities in prison construction are even worse than with hospitals. The government finds itself criticized from start to finish. Local people are up in arms at the thought of a prison being constructed in their midst, but eventually, as communities become dependent upon the monthly payroll, they protest any attempt to close the institution.

There is an important difference between shutting down an older prison and declaring an entire system bankrupt. The latter requires a conceptual breakthrough of a very high order. It cannot happen overnight. There must be a long period of gestation in which a full realization of the extent and consequences of the failure become apparent. There must be books, articles, TV specials that expose the scandals and corruption to highlight the continuing inability of the institution to fulfill its purposes. I am not sure that we have reached this point in the history of imprisonment, but we are close to it. It has taken two centuries of criticism, from Charles Dickens to today's abolitionists, to shift the focus of discussion away from prisons as buildings and on to imprisonment as a social policy. The abandonment of imprisonment will not automatically take us back to flogging, dunking, and the gallows. The rejection of a lesser evil does not require us to accept a greater one; we may want to take a second look at banishment and ridicule (social pressure) as these methods are practiced in socialist countries.

But most difficult of all will be to face the issue of social justice in America. If the nation is willing to exclude millions of citizens from the mainstream of society, denying them dignity and the opportunity to lead productive lives, there can be no real reform of the criminal justice system. Without economic and political justice, we will only substitute one ineffective and immoral method of punishment for another. The only way to reduce crime is to eliminate its roots in poverty, racism, and elitism. By elitism is meant the belief that only a chosen few deserve to succeed and that their success is due to their own innate abilities. This is to condemn millions of citizens who are not terribly bright or agile to half-lives on welfare or in institutions. American society will have to begin caring about students who are being pushed out of traditional schools. What is clear is that society must care about all its children, not merely those who score the highest marks on multiple-choice examinations and fit the cultural stereotype of success. A humane society cannot condemn tens of millions to be losers. The nation's vast correctional apparatus is one of several repositories for those failures. It does not take great imagination to list dozens of jobs that a mentally retarded person can perform. Studies have shown that mental imbeciles, people with IQs between 25 and 50, can perform industrial tasks efficiently, provided the tasks are programmed into small, discreet, manageable steps.[11] The problem is not one of redefining mental deficiency but of finding reasonable niches for all citizens. The ideology of reform (corrections) is predicated upon the notion that most human beings, even those who have broken the law, are improvable to some degree. The problem faced by the correctional system is not so much the premise itself but the methods used to reform people. It has become apparent that imprisonment is an extremely ineffective way of accomplishing reform. It is probably the worst method imaginable.

Who Is a Political Prisoner?

This is one of the great non-issues of our time. Before deciding who is a political prisoner, we must first define political imprisonment; then we can decide who fits this category. It quickly becomes apparent that defining political imprisonment makes the second step unnecessary. There are so many connections between imprisonment and the American political system that no separation of the two is possible.

Judges are elected themselves or appointed by elected officials. Their appointments are tied closely to the party system and political ideology.

Criminal acts are defined by elected legislators or by officials in the executive branch who are ultimately responsible to an elected official. The definition of crime, the enforcement of laws, and the nature of penalties are determined by whichever group is in power.

Parole boards are appointed by elected officials and their decisions are heavily influenced by political loyalties.

Elected officials and legislative bodies affect the criminal justice system through the budget allocation process. They can control attempts to build new prisons or shut down obsolete ones. Often a candidate will run for office on a law-and-order platform.

The power of investigation is another of the levers that the legislature has over the prison system. Exposure of corruption is a recurring theme in American politics.

In theory, no one can be imprisoned in this country for his or her political beliefs. However, the expression of those beliefs in times of crisis can lead to harassment, arrest, and imprisonment.

Race, social class, and urbanicity are significantly related to crime, arrest, and imprisonment. These factors correlate with political affiliation. Any attempt to change the criminal justice system will have different effects upon the various social classes, ethnic groups, and political parties.

It is easy to document similar degrees of political influence on all social institutions, including health care and environmental affairs. It would be redundant to preface every role, status, or policy with the term "political." We would have "political doctors" and "political patients," "political teachers" and "political students," as well as "political judges," "political police," and "political prisoners." This kind of verbiage can have educational value in conveying the connection between, for example, politics and the school system, but it can conceivably have the reverse effect. Using the phrase "political teacher" implies that it is possible to be a *non*political teacher; the phrase "political prisoner" implies that it is possible to be a prisoner whose incarceration is not affected by the political process. The very redundancy of "political" everything would soon dissipate its meaning. It would be more effective to recognize the political aspects of all social institutions, including the criminal justice system, than to compound words into meaninglessness.

Real progress will require abandoning idealistic thinking in favor of an ecological view of crime. We will have to look at the conditions that encourage crime rather than looking solely at the people unfortunate enough to get caught. It is clear that the correlates of crime are age, ethnicity, urbanicity, gender, and lack of employment. We can continue to blame crime upon young, urban, uneducated, and unskilled minority males and put them into institutions where they will be further corrupted, stigmatized, and demeaned, or we can attempt to eliminate chronic unemployment, inadequate housing, unresponsive schools, and the success ethic that dooms tens of millions to be failures. Idealistic thinking ends up heaping further abuse on those already fallen. The ecological approach would have us alter those conditions which produce and perpetuate criminal behavior.

MOCK INSTITUTIONS AND IMPERSONATIONS 6

There seems to be no doubt that APEX simulates reality for some players, even in a short-lived demonstration. "It's painfully close to the bone," said a dazed role-playing city politician, a man who actually works on the staff of New York City's administrator for environmental protection. "APEX has all the frustrations of the real city government. You can't get anything done. No one listens to you. You can't get money for programs. And you have to make decisions without nearly enough time or information."

When a real-life situation gets too hot to handle, it is necessary to back off and view it at a distance. If there is time, it will be useful to develop a simulated reality which can be experimentally altered. This does not mean substituting fantasy for reality, or converting people into abstractions, but rather going one step further than the model formation described in Chapter 2 and testing various methods in a systematic fashion. Simulations are helpful in situations where the usual means of gaining information through interviews and direct observation won't work. Talking with inmates and guards, visiting prisons, and analyzing parole and recidivism statistics all produce a tremendous frustration and despair. Every participant in this miasma of failure has a reasonable defense of his or her actions. A laboratory simulation of the basic processes can go beyond individual personalities and long-standing disputes. It is not suggested that the laboratory prison is an exact replica of a real prison, but only that we may learn something about the processes of imprisonment that is not easily observed or verified in real jails dominated by distrust and acrimony. Some of the shortcomings of simulations and role-playing exercises will be discussed at the conclusion of this chapter.

There are situations, such as jury deliberations, where direct observation is unethical and illegal, and the best available method to gather information is simulation. The issue must be faced of whether artificial jury deliberations are indeed similar to actual ones. Bermant et al. presented four groups of undergraduate students with different amounts of information about an actual murder trial that took place in Detroit and ended in a verdict of manslaughter. The four groups received information in decreasing degrees of structural resemblance to an actual jury trial. Group 1, with maximum verisimilitude, observed a fifty-minute automated slide show showing people in the courtroom acting the roles of judge, prosecutor, defense attorney, defendant, witnesses, courtroom audience, and court reporter. At the end of the trial, individuals were asked for individual verdicts, then formed into juries for group decisions, and then once again asked for individual verdicts. Group 2 heard an audio tape without any slides. Group 3 read a thirty-page transcript of the audio tape, and Group 4 received a four-page summary of the evidence and the judge's instructions with no group decisions required. Paradoxically, Bermant found that the groups that had the most information available also had the highest proportion of students voting for acquittal! The conviction rate was highest in the group that had only the four-page summary and the judge's instructions.[1] It must be remembered that the actual verdict in this case was for a manslaughter conviction. Therefore, the greater the degree of structural verisimilitude, the less well these results resembled those of an actual jury. However, the conclusions from this single experiment should not be overgeneralized; perhaps the actual jury in this case was mistaken and the simulated jury with the video presentation was correct. Still experiments like this make us aware of the dangers of generalizing directly from a simulation exercise to a real-world situation.

There are numerous sorts of artificial realities. Systems theorists distinguish between *replications, simulations,* and *formalizations*. A replication possesses a high degree of structural resemblence to the object or system being modeled, e.g. a model airplane. A simulation depends less on structural resemblance than on functional resemblance, i.e. the useful equivalence of its conditions to those of the object being modeled. Formalizations, which include the broad category of mathematical models, aim more for logical consistency than for perceptual likeness.[2] *Experimental games* fall somewhere between simulations and formalizations. *Impersonation* represents the intrusion of a mock role player into a real situation.

The experimental summer camps run by Muzafer and Carolyn Sherif illustrate the use of simulation in conflict reduction.[3] Early in the school year the Sherifs contacted families in the New Haven area in order to locate children who wanted to attend a summer camp sponsored by Yale University. From those who volunteered, the Sherifs selected normal, healthy children from various parts of the city who had not known one another before. Almost as soon as the children settled into the camp, they formed cliques and gangs based on dormitory assignments. They took on nicknames (Red Devils and Bulldogs), made insignias, and coined slogans. When the gangs came into conflict as a result of circumstances created by the experimenters, these same normal and healthy youngsters improvised weapons which they concealed "in case they were needed," raided one another's cabins, tore down opposition banners, and threw plates and silverware during numerous dining room squabbles. Each group assigned negative stereotypes to its rival which served to justify its own actions. These negative stereotypes were not the initial causes of the dispute, but were an outcome of the intergroup rivalry. However, once stereotypes were formed, they provided a rationalization for hostile and aggressive actions. Small misunderstandings, in several cases orchestrated by staff, escalated into a vicious circle of hostile encounters, each side justifying its actions and blaming the other for what happened. The Sherifs point out that individual gang members need not be neurotic or sinful for such a vicious circle to develop. The Sherifs found that neither persuasion nor administrative punishment could end the dispute. It was necessary to evolve superordinate goals which were outcomes desired by all parties and which could not be achieved by the actions of any single party separately, but only through their combined efforts. A series of encounters involving superordinate goals was necessary in order for the hostilities to be replaced by friendly or neutral cooperation. Several large-scale actions provided the basis for frequent person-to-person contacts, information exchanges, and conferences between group leaders. These results support the GRIT theory of tension reduction developed by Charles Osgood, involving small step-by-step unilateral moves intended to bring about reciprocity.[4] A formalization rather than a simulation, GRIT tries to reverse the usual sequence of graduated increments of hostile responses which tend to be reciprocated ad infinitum. Instead, Osgood proposes small unilateral conciliatory moves, each preceded by an announcement and carried out without any degree of reciprocity. A succession of such moves, none really sacrificing the security of the participants, will, in Osgood's view, lead to a reversal of mutual tension and deadlock. At least, it will help to develop the backdrop of trust and hope to encourage negotiations for further measures to reduce tensions. The Osgood approach requires some reciprocity in making concessions. It is not simply one side conceding small items until it has nothing more left with which to bargain. Either side may begin with one or two unilateral tension-reducing measures, but if there is no reciprocation, the approach must be held in abeyance until a more propitious time. Obviously this method cannot be used when only one side has something with which to bargain.

The GRIT formalization and the simulated conflict created by the

Sherifs involve conflict between peers. While they may have some value for understanding and resolving violence within the inmate society, they are not relevant to guard-prisoner interaction. To learn about behavior in a situation of great power inequality, we will turn next to a specific attempt to simulate imprisonment.

The Stanford County Jail

In 1971 Philip Zimbardo created an artificial prison in the basement of the Stanford University Psychology Building.[5] College students were recruited through ads in a Palo Alto newspaper offering $15 a day to people who would participate in a two-week study of prison life. All volunteers were carefully screened to eliminate anyone with serious psychological problems, medical disabilities, a history of crime or drug abuse, or any other specific pathology. This left twenty-four volunteers who were all students from colleges across the country. A flip of the coin decided whether a volunteer would be a prisoner or a guard. At the outset the two groups were similar in all respects.

Zimbardo constructed a mock prison with the advice of several ex-convicts and law enforcement people. Everything possible was done to make the situation realistic. When he was not able to be literal, e.g. shave the heads of the "prisoners," Zimbardo used symbolic substitutes, such as requiring the prisoners to wear stocking caps that gave the appearance of shaved heads. Each prisoner was arrested in his home by the city police, frisked, blindfolded, and driven in a real police car to the real Palo Alto jail for processing, before being taken later to the mock basement prison. Then followed a series of procedures designed to convey to the prisoner his inferior status and the control of his life by the authorities. The prisoner was stripped, deloused, assigned a number that replaced his name, and compelled to wear a heavy chain at all times. Prisoners and guards were assigned uniforms that submerged individuality and developed anonymity. Guards' uniforms consisted of plain khaki shirts and trousers, a whistle, a wooden baton, and reflecting sunglasses that made eye contact impossible. Inmates' uniforms consisted of loose-fitting muslin smocks with numbers stenciled in front and back, no underclothes underneath these ''dresses,'' and stocking caps over their heads. The prisoners' attire was specifically designed to degrade them and underline their helplessness.

The degradation ceremonies were effective in changing the demeanor of the ''prisoners'' from that of intellectually alert young people to that of servile, withdrawn, and seemingly sub-human creatures. Guards became autocratic and in some cases brutal in enforcing rules and occasionally inventing their own. The experiment, which was supposed to run two weeks, was abruptly terminated after six days because of the damage it was doing to prisoners, guards, and the experimenters themselves. Four prisoners had to be discharged when they showed extreme emotional reactions, and virtually all the other prisoners were showing the strain. Some guards had become sadistic; even the ''good guards'' felt helpless to do anything about their brutal colleagues and watched helplessly while inmates were being pushed around. An ex-convict who was brought in to preside at a parole board hearing found himself impersonating the officials who had turned him down repeatedly. During the parole hearing, each inmate was offered his parole if he would be willing to forfeit the promised $15 a day. All but two of the prisoners readily accepted the offer, even though it seemingly negated all of the reasons for their having endured this torture. They had come to accept ther role as prisoners with no rights. Even the families of the ''prisoners'' accepted their own subservient status vis-à-vis the experimenters. Zimbardo found himself losing his detachment as a psychologist and becoming the warden he was impersonating. He was more concerned with security than with the welfare of the students for whom he had become responsible. When he realized this, Zimbardo terminated the experiment, which had succeeded only too well in mimicking the oppression of the prison.

Personality tests had been given to guards and inmates at various times and detailed recordings were made of people's reactions. The tests showed that there were no differences between inmates and guards in their adjustment beforehand, and all were in the normal range of personality stability. However, both groups became very negative during the course of the experiment both in outlook and in expressed intention to harm others. Although inmates and guards had been free to engage in any kind of interaction, positive or negative, negative encounters tended to predominate. The most frequent kind of verbal contact from the guards was a command, and conversations, when they did occur, tended to be impersonal. Although the experimenter had specifically excluded any kind of physical violence, many aggressive encounters did take place, mostly initiated by the guards.

The most dramatic evidence of the prison's impact on the inmates was the early discharge of the four inmates who showed extreme emotional responses. When Zimbardo described their behavior to staff and inmates at Rhode Island State Prison, he was informed that the Stanford County Jail had produced a *first-offender reaction*. People breaking down, weeping, and getting skin rashes are more common in juvenile institutions and jails than in prisons, where inmates have traveled the institutional route and learned to control their emotions. All the remaining prisoners in Zimbardo's jail were delighted when the study was terminated, but most of the guards were distressed. They did not want to relinquish the authority which had become so satisfying for them. Most of the private conversations of the participants concerned the immediate prison conditions. Prisoners talked about food, harassment, and privileges. Guards talked about "problem prisoners" or did not talk at all.

For ethical reasons Zimbardo did not simulate the most despicable aspects of the prison system—the racism, sadism, and lethal violence. Even the minimal conditions used were sufficient to provoke the most extreme responses from students who had been selected because of their demonstrated healthiness and emotional stability. There is no possibility of explaining these results on the basis of the previous pathology of the participants, as the dispositional hypothesis attempts to do. According to this hypothesis, brutallty is the result of guards who are sadistic, uneducated, and insensitive, and inmates who are impulsive, aggressive, and disrespectful of law.[6] Though not every inmate or guard has these negative characteristics, there are enough "bad apples" to spoil both barrels. This view also maintains that recognition of the authoritarian nature of the institution attracts sadistic, autocratic people into prison work. In few other jobs can a relatively uneducated and untalented individual enjoy such absolute authority over other human beings. The inmates are not "selected" for the prison in the same way as the guards, and they don't "choose" to come to prison, but they are drawn to it by a persistent history of aggressiveness, impulsiveness, and failure. The prison is the natural repository of losers. Given the preponderance of these kinds of people, it is not surprising, according to the dispositional hypothesis, that prisons are brutal and oppressive places. Austin MacCormick, one of the most distinguished figures in American penology, declared, "If only I had the right staff, I could run a good prison in an old red barn." [7] If one takes this statement at face value, MacCormack is attributing the deficiencies of the prison to the wrong kind of staff. It would also be possible to change the statement around to say, "If only I had the right inmates, I could run a good prison in an old red barn." Think of what could be done if one had the right staff and the right inmates! The fallacy of the dispositional hypothesis, and of all such purely psychological explanations, is that they overlook the situational constraints. The right kind of people can be ground to bits in the wrong kind of institution.

The dispositional hypothesis also produces the blame syndrome discussed earlier. Fortunately a simulation exercise cuts through the hypothesis and allows us to separate individuals from social roles. Who is to "blame" for the sadistic behavior of the Stanford guards? Is their sadism the result of faulty parental practices, of a school system that fosters blind obedience to authority, of the psychology department which provided the facilities for the research, or of Philip Zimbardo who designed the study? In this case, we can state specifically that the guards' sadism resulted from their roles in the miniprison. We can express some surprise at how quickly their good intentions and humane values deteriorated. Perhaps a different sort of school system would have strengthened them against the temptation to dominate and dehumanize, but it doesn't seem likely. These volunteers came from colleges all around the country, and they were selected as being relatively free from neurotic tendencies. There is as much logic in blaming these students as there is in blaming their parents for raising their children as they did. With a simulation there is always the master villain, the simulator himself—in this case Philip Zimbardo. In actuality, Zimbardo has come under fire, not only from the public, but also from his own colleagues, for his handling of the experiment and even for undertaking it. To blame Zimbardo seems a further manifestation of psychological reductionism, in which the image rather than the reality of prison becomes the problem. To be sure, there are legitimate ethical issues connected with Zimbardo's handling of the Stanford jail, but we cannot let them sidetrack us from a discussion of the very real effects of jails upon inmates and staff.

Weekend at Elgin

Twenty-nine staff members at Elgin State Hospital spent a three-day holiday weekend living as patients on a mental ward. Twenty-two of their fellow employees spent the weekend simulating the role of staff members. The experiment was done by Irma Jean Orlando to see if the results of the Zimbardo experiment would be found on a simulated mental ward.[8] All the participants, both patients and staff, were volunteers, mostly young (the average age was twenty-four), but there were some in their forties and fifties. The simulated patients lived on a hospital ward but were not in contact with genuine patients except at mealtimes. Everyone, staff and patients alike, dined in the hospital cafeteria. The admissions procedure was the start of a series of assaults upon the patient's dignity. Following an intake interview, the patient was escorted to the clothing room, where ill-fitting state garments were issued, which included "scuffies," an item associated with low status, wrong-sized underwear, and pants held up with shoe strings. Following the required shower, patients were stripped of their own clothing and given a detailed body check by a staff member, and a record of their belongings was made on a printed form before the belongings were taken away. The patients were taken to the ward, where they were introduced by name to the staff but not vice versa. As in the Zimbardo study, the staff wore reflecting sunglasses, which made it impossible for the patients to maintain eye contact. There were periodic medication sessions in which the patients received placebos (sugar pills). Attempts were made to create a crowded atmosphere; the dayroom and the dormitory were small and the patients were not allowed into the dormitory during the day. All recreation took place in the small dayroom. The negative effects of the lack of chairs in the dayroom were compounded by rules that patients could not sit or lie on the floor. The toilets were not private, and there were bed checks of the patients at night. The staff deliberately attempted to dehumanize the patients by discussing their personal problems among themselves in full hearing of the patients. While Zimbardo had used numbers for his inmates, these patients were given new names. Special requests by the patients were often answered, ''If I let you do it, then everyone else will want to do it.'' Generally the staff feigned disinterest in the patient's personal situation.

These measures proved effective in demoralizing the patients. Some were found pacing back and forth, while others sat mute in the available chairs, looking down at the floor or staring at a blank wall. A few rather extreme reactions occurred, but, perhaps because the time was half that of the Stanford experiment and because there were more people around, the proportion of hysterical reactions was less than in the mock jail. Several patients attempted to escape from the ward, broke windows, and stole not only from the staff but from other patients, and there was one fistfight between a patient and a staff member over administration of ''medication.'' Several of the patients, but none of the staff, wept uncontrollably at times. Tension on the ward kept rising, and at least one patient expressed fear of having an actual breakdown.

Everyone filled out a brief questionnaire just before the announcement that the experiment was over. There was unanimity among the patients about feeling ignored, dehumanized, and rejected. Debriefing sessions were held to enable people to express their feelings. The statements of the pseudopatients parallel criticisms made by actual patients:

> Felt at the mercy of personalities. No recourse.
>
> Patients have no power; can't make decisions.
>
> Felt labelled as a troublemaker because of asking for a simple thing. Can't understand rules.
>
> Everything was the patient's fault. No way to let out hostility. Couldn't concentrate. Still upset about clothes on Saturday morning. Staff didn't give a shit how you looked or how you felt.
>
> Meals—we knew the food was bad; worst was way it was served. Didn't have an appetite. Didn't always have fork; knives and spoons not there.
>
> No time orientation. Repression, lack of privacy, feeling like an object, feeling delusional, feeling of no value, because of staff attitude.

While no one had to be released early because of an hysterical breakdown, there was enough pathology to suggest that the conditions of the mock ward were extremely oppressive. The experimenter concluded that many of the behaviors of actual mental patients, including withdrawal, anxiety, and anger, are produced by the ward environment itself. Confinement in a mental institution can in itself "increase the psychopathology and the deterioration of an already disturbed individual." The evidence is overwhelming that mental patients, even those who are withdrawn and seemingly apathetic, are not insensitive to their surroundings. Indeed, as Orlando argues, much of the withdrawal and the apathy may be the result of boring, sterile, and dehumanizing ward conditions. Whether or not this is intended, the typical ward routine is demeaning to the patient's individuality and unsuited to preparing the patient for taking control over his or her life after release.

"Doc Cop"

Impersonation is another means of making an experimental probe into an institution. Instead of constructing an artificial world and using volunteer actors, the researcher becomes a mock employee or mock client of an actual institution. This has been a favorite tactic of field researchers, who call it *participant observation*. Rather than remaining a passive onlooker or interviewer, the participant observer actively plays one of the available roles. This approach comes under fire from colleagues who believe that assuming a real role will result in a loss of objectivity. Acknowledging some legitimacy to this criticism, field researchers maintain that their firsthand access to data outweighs the potential biases. Field researchers also doubt that any observer can maintain complete detachment and objectivity in a stressful situation and say that their own biases are "on the table" for everyone to take into account. Another ethical issue concerns the amount of knowledge that others have of the impersonation. This has varied greatly from one study to the next. William Caudill, a young anthropologist, had himself admitted to a mental hospital as a pseudopatient.[9] His impersonation was known to the top administration of the hospital but not to the ward staff or his fellow patients. Sociologist Laud Humphreys impersonated a "watch queen" to observe homosexual encounters in public restrooms where none of the participants (or the authorities) were aware of his research interest.[10] Sociologist Sherri Cavan worked as a cocktail waitress in order to study bars in San Francisco.[11] Criminologist George Kirkham took a year's leave from his university position to go through training in a police academy and work as a patrolman. Many of his fellow officers were aware of his research interests (his nickname was "Doc"), but the people on his beat looked upon him as an ordinary policeman. Kirkham writes with great sensitivity of the changes in his own attitudes that took place as he worked a high-crime neighborhood.

> According to the accounts of my family, colleagues, and friends, I began to increasingly display attitudinal and behavioral elements that were entirely foreign to my previous personality—punitiveness, pervasive cynicism and mistrust of others, chronic irritiability and free-floating hostility, racism, and a diffuse personal anxiety over the menace of crime and criminals that seemed at times to border on the obsessive.[12]

In his role as policeman, he became a vociferous advocate of capital punishment even though, as a criminologist, he acknowledged its ineffectiveness as a deterrent. He also became a strong advocate of retribution and resented the courts' "coddling" of criminals. His inability to reconcile his conflicting perspectives began to seem like hypocrisy. He began to have doubts about which was the real George Kirkham. The answer, he acknowledged, was in the situations in which he found himself. It was much easier to be detached and objective sitting in an office or around a seminar table with a group of students and colleagues than as a policemen in direct contact with violence.

Sharing the risks with his fellow officers gave Kirkham insights that he felt could not have been obtained through interviews or questionnaires. The hyperaggressiveness and braggadocio of his fellow officers began to make sense as a collective defense mechanism. Any show of weakness on the part of one patrolman threatened the entire force. Kirkham left his beat after a year's service and returned to a placid existence as a university professor. Unanswered questions impelled him to embark on an additional six-month stint as a policeman in a small community with very little crime. The tension and hostility of the previous job was absent. He could come home and take off his badge and uniform with "a new and far deeper feeling of service and satisfaction."

There have not been serious criticisms of Kirkham's research on ethical grounds. Since he went through the regular police academy training and passed all the tests, he was obviously well qualified for the job. Impersonation has not been done in prisons very often. Occasionally a group of judges or lawyers will spend a night in jail to see what it is like. In most every case the staff and the other inmates are aware of their identities even if they try to conceal them.

Rosenhan's Pseudopatients

Impersonation has been more frequently practiced in mental institutions. For one thing it is much easier to go in and out. One of the most controversial such experiments was staged by Stanford professor David Rosenhan and seven of his friends, who had themselves admitted to various kinds of mental hospitals, including old and new, public and private, custodial and research-oriented institutions.[13] They wanted to find out if the staff would recognize them as sane people. Each person presented himself at the hospital admission desk with the general story that he was hearing voices which were often unclear, which seemed to say "empty," "hollow," and "thud." This was supposed to portray an existential psychosis which Rosenhan had *never* seen mentioned in psychiatric literature. Once the patient was admitted, the simulation ceased, and everything the patient said to the staff was accurate.

This study is valuable because it shows us how men and women change into patients once they enter a mental hospital. The pseudopatients began to behave as they were treated. Their actions were constantly distorted and misinterpreted by the staff. The pseudopatient who paced the corridor out of boredom was regarded by the nurses as nervous. Note-taking was labeled as "writing behavior" and considered a pathological symptom. Patients waiting outside the cafeteria a half hour before lunchtime were described as exhibiting "oral acquisitive symptoms." Everything the patient did and said was judged in the light of the initial diagnosis. When the pseudopatients were discharged, at their own request, the label used in seven out of eight cases was "schizophrenia in remission." Like Zimbardo, Rosenhan did not feel that the staff's insensitivity to the pseudopatients was a result of deliberate malice or stupidity. The overwhelming impression of his observers was that the staff were people who really cared, were highly motivated in their work, and of high intelligence and integrity. The culprit in his eyes is the method of global diagnosis and labeling that conditions staff to see illness in reasonable adaptations to an unnatural environment. These labels act as self-fulfilling prophecies that should be replaced, Rosenhan believes, by terms which more descriptively fit tangible behaviors. Rosenhan later attempted to repeat this experiment in a jail, but the entire experience was too stressful, and the impersonations terminated.

The Ethics of Simulation

It can be argued that there is no reason to simulate prisons or hospitals when it is possible to interview prisoners and patients and observe the real thing. Unfortunately such situations are so polarized and fraught with paleologic that the opinions of those directly concerned are invariably dismissed as biased and self-serving by those of opposing views. Observation of prisons by outsiders is prevented by administrative edict. Given these obstacles to research in actual prisons, and the difficulties in disentangling problems from history, politics, and ego, there is some value in laboratory simulation. It can also eliminate the selection bias inherent in natural situations. A simulation exercise can help test the dispositional hypothesis by placing people of equivalent dispositions in various critical roles.

I will mention another simulation exercise that did not, as far as I know, arouse any criticism at all. Herbert Leiderman recruited a group of healthy volunteers willing to be confined in a respirator for thirty-six hours. "All reported difficulties in concentration, periodic anxiety feelings, and a loss of ability to judge time. Eight . . . reported some distortions of reality ranging from pseudosomatic delusions to frank visual hallucinations. Four subjects terminated the experiment because of anxiety; two of these in panic tried to release themselves forcibly from the respirator." [14] As far as I know, no one has characterized this experiment as sensational or unethical, even though none of the volunteers needed a respirator. Leiderman's results show the need to compensate for the impoverished environment of the respirator and of the likely pathologies if this is not done. No longer can the apathy of some respirator patients be attributed solely to their physical maladies. The use of healthy volunteers instead of sick people produces an artificial situation, but this helps to separate outcomes from pre-existing morbid conditions.

Impersonation experiments encounter the criticism that a person cannot be both a sociologist and an actor in a real-life drama. Anyone who can return to the security of the university after a short stint cannot inhabit the same psychological space as a policeman, skid row alcoholic, or hospital attendant. There are also serious ethical problems when many of the people involved do not know that their lives are being captured in the sociologist's notebook. I find these objections less than compelling. One can learn a great deal more about a situation when one is subject to the same risks, even for short periods, as the other people in it.

When I discuss the Zimbardo experiment with my students, two objections are raised. The first concerns the ethics of the research. How could Zimbardo have permitted so many students to break down before stopping the experiment? Couldn't he have seen what was coming when the second student had an hysterical outburst? Students complain that Zimbardo was too close to his experiment to be objective. There should have been someone less detached and less personally involved monitoring the whole process, some kind of ombudsman. Zimbardo admits to having been caught up in his role as commissioner. I would applaud his honesty in admitting this involvement rather than trying to cover it up. This experiment had never been tried before, and Zimbardo had no way of predicting what would happen. The possibility that a group of young people preselected as to their mental health would break down in this pale copy of a jail was totally unanticipated. Zimbardo and his colleagues spent a lot of time with the students afterwards, both inmates and guards, discussing what happened and working through their feelings about their participation. We can hope that there are no long-range ill effects upon the participants. Zimbardo's honest report of what happened suggests that it would be unwise and unethical to repeat the experiment without stronger safeguards for the well-being of the participants.

Paradoxically, the second line of criticism concerns the realism of the procedure. Students simply cannot believe that an effective simulation of a jail could be staged in the basement of a psychology building. They insist that everybody must have been playing at their roles. The implication is that it would have been more effective to conduct the experiment in a vacant wing of Attica. Instead of college students, we could hire twelve unemployed blacks from Harlem to be inmates and twelve part-time farmers or factory workers from rural areas of upstate New York as guards. At this point the line between simulation and reality would be tenuous. We could also hire ex-cons to be prisoners again, and pay regular prison guards to work an additional shift in a mock prison, and have everybody exchange roles at midpoint. And when we tire of constructing dream worlds, we can always return to the steel and concrete reality of the prison.

SHOWCASE PRISONS 7

The Case of the Watergate Inmates

> *Prisoners in the Tarrant City Jail get only two meals a day unless they're on a work gang. They get no meat, only water to drink with each meal, and are sometimes served TV dinners on holidays. Summing up his response to the complaints, Mayor Evan Veal said, "We're not fixing to change it. As far as the prisoners are concerned, they can stay out of our jail and they won't have to eat our unpalatable food."*

Most reform proposals recommend building nicer prisons which should be as non-institutional as possible. These non-prisons should be small, modern, close to the inmate's home, provide decent medical and dental care, and have counseling and vocational programs available on a voluntary basis and ample recreational facilities. These suggestions stem from a reform model, which can be contrasted to the deterrent/retribution position of keeping prisons as unpleasant places which people should try to stay out of. Due to the different models being employed, it is not likely that the disagreement between these two positions can be settled through argument. Fortunately, there are some natural experiments available that can provide pertinent data. There exist what most people would call nice prisons. This description is apt for the showcase federal facilities at Allenwood, Pennsylvania, and Lompoc, California, along with a few state facilities for juveniles. Through the historical accident of the Watergate scandals, the American public has been given a searching look inside these institutions.*

Unlike most convicted offenders, who are lost from view once they enter prison, the spotlight of publicity continued to fall upon the Watergate inmates. The interviews and articles in newspapers and on TV were virtually unprecedented in the federal penal system, where people change almost immediately from names to numbers. Even the simultaneous incarceration at Allenwood a few years ago of such notables as Bobby Baker, Carmine DeSapio, General Carl Turner, Clifford Irving, and Ralph Ginzburg did not arouse the media to such a degree. Such notorious figures as Sirhan Sirhan, Charles Manson, and James Earl Ray disappeared from public view behind prison walls. Proponents of prison reform have viewed the publicity given the Watergate inmates with mixed emotions.

Without exception the major Watergate figures were sent or were scheduled to go to the showcase federal institutions. Their sentences were extraordinarily light compared to those given other offenders. They were all big shots, and traditionally big shots have special handling in prison. According to the accounts of guards, Lucky Luciano was the most important person in Dannemora State Penitentiary. ''He practically ran the place,'' a guard reported. ''He used to stand there in the yard like he was the warden. Men waited in line to talk with him. Charlie Lucky would listen, say something, then wave his hand. The guy would actually *back* away.'' Former Teamsters president Jimmy Hoffa describes the power he possessed in Lewisburg Prison where he spent five years: ''Drivers came into the yard from outside, they'd lean out the window, yell up at the prison windows, 'Hey Jim!

* The details of Watergate pertinent to this section are given in the Background Note at the end of this chapter.

Good Luck!' If anyone tried to shove *me* in the hole, the trucks would stop delivering.'' [1]

The benign policies of these institutions extend to generous visiting policies, periodic furloughs, access to telephones and mailboxes, and decent food. While inmates of other institutions are unanimous in their criticism of the tasteless, ill-prepared, unrecognizable, and non-nutritious ''slop,'' men at Lompoc and Allenwood are very complimentary. By coincidence, these are the prisons most accessible to outside journalists and TV reporters. Father Philip Berrigan, who spent time at Allenwood for his anti-war activities, was rhapsodic in his description of the Allenwood food.

> In terms of substance and nutrition, always superb. Many of their own vegetables were grown right in the area; you get fresh vegetables and tomatoes during the summer. The meat, even though it was only served once a day and in limited quantities, would be excellent; fine pork and beef, and in some cases even steak, since they were raising their own cattle. You would have some milk, there would be fruit juice. And of course the prisoners did the baking, and the baked goods would be excellent. The bread was almost Trappist-like in its quality and content, and of all descriptions: white bread, whole wheat, rye, and really superior buns from time to time for breakfast. Twice a week you would get eggs, and their own home-grown bacon. Other times you would have a pick of good dry cereal, or substantial oatmeal (for breakfast). So the food, by and large, I would say, was excellent.[2]

Newly built prisons attempt to avoid the mass-feeding problems of the older places by locating smaller dining halls within individual living units. This also permits some variation in diet and the preparation of special menus such as those for Muslims, who do not eat pork products. However the stratified prison system operates in such a way that those inmates from low-income areas who have been on starvation diets much of their lives go to maximum-security institutions with the worst food, and the white-collar inmates such as embezzlers or Watergate conspirators go to showcase institutions with excellent food. This makes no sense from the standpoint of equal justice for all, deterrence, or reform.

Role of the Media

Until Watergate the maximum-security places such as Sing Sing and Jackson received virtually all the press coverage on the prison beat. Scores of entertainers came to San Quentin to stage a gala New Year's show, and big-name bands gave concerts. The publicity surrounding these events and the romanticized version of prison life on TV depicted the prison as a place of high walls, steel bars, and armed guards stationed around the clock in gun towers. As an aftermath of Watergate the public was suddenly given a glimpse of a very different sort of environment—open, verdant, with ample sports facilities and a minimum of restrictions. To a degree, this was a healthy corrective to the popular stereotype of prison, since a sizable number of state and federal institutions are minimum-security facilities, more like Allenwood than San Quentin.

The penetration of the media into the federal prison system, perhaps the deepest penetration ever accomplished by television and the press, is a hopeful portent. The question is whether this can be continued and extended to other institutions and other inmates. Reporters who visited the minimum-security camp at Lompoc ignored the nearby federal medium-security facility with its predominantly black and brown lower-class inmate population. Nor have the reporters covering Magruder and Krogh at Allenwood seen fit to visit the maximum security-Lewisburg Penitentiary eighteen miles away. Publicity has come to those institutions most likely to raise charges of "coddling convicts." There has been very little penetration of the institutions where the greatest violence has occurred. According to journalist Tom Wicker, "The greatest overall deficiency of the American press is that it relies too much on official sources. Nowhere is this deficiency more evident than in routine prison coverage, when there is any." [3] This gap in reporting is not necessarily the fault of the press. Correctional authorities routinely deny reporters and photographers access to maximum-security institutions on the grounds of the reporters' safety and the inmates' privacy. Both reasons are specious and self-serving. If reporters can volunteer for the front lines in Korea and Vietnam, they could undoubtedly survive in maximum-security (!) institutions. Particularly during times of stress, inmates have asked for more rather than less press coverage to protect their rights. Opening up prisons to round-the-clock media coverage may not solve all the prisons' problems, but it would prevent the more obvious brutality and help prepare the public for meaningful change. The constant television reporting of the bombing and artillery fire in Vietnam and the frequent atrocities increased the public revulsion at that immoral war. It is likely that first-hand reporting of conditions in Jackson would raise public consciousness and reduce the more blatant atrocities.

The prison wall keeps the public out as well as the inmates in. The rules governing visits to most prisons for families as well as interested persons are petty and humiliating. For me as a college teacher, the contrast between a class tour of a mental hospital and one of a prison is striking. Let me use the example of a nearby penal institution which is euphemistically called the California Medical Facility, since authorities claim that the institution is a type of mental hospital. One would not therefore expect a great difference in one's reception at the medical facility and at a nearby mental hospital.

A tour of the mental hospital is comparatively easy to arrange. One makes an appointment beforehand with the volunteer coordinator, and, upon arriving on the grounds, goes to his or her office, obtains the services of several patients who will act as guides, takes a tour through the wards, and then departs. Things are very different at the "Medical Facility." Telephone inquiries get nowhere. A letter to the superintendent eventually produces a form letter and two pages of requirements and rules. The most difficult requirement is that we must find an employee who is willing to take responsibility for us and show us around. This, of course, has to be someone with enough status to alter his schedule or who is willing to conduct a tour on his free time. Names of all the people on the proposed tour must be cleared in advance with prison authorities. The purpose of this requirement is to screen out any ex-convicts, so it must be assumed that all these names are put through the state computers. Visitors are not allowed to wear blue jeans or "provocative clothing" or to carry handbags or, of course, cameras. Nor are visitors allowed to engage in casual conversation with inmates. Assuming that they meet all these requirements, visitors must sign in, have their hands stamped with a special ink, and empty their pockets of all metal before walking through the magnetometer and the various locked doors, gates, and sally ports. The tour is restricted to those areas most designed to impress visitors.

The treatment of the inmate's family is even more degrading. Skin searches of visitors are likely to occur and, depending upon circumstances, the inmate and the visitor may be separated by wire mesh and required to converse through an intercom.

Dickinson surveyed sixty-four state prisons in 1971 as to their policies regarding correspondence, visiting, and use of telephone by inmates.[4] He found that 42 per cent of the institutions limited the number of letters an inmate was allowed to write; the most common reason for this restriction was to reduce the volume of mail that had to be inspected. To justify the censorship, 59 per cent of the prisons asked the inmate upon admission to sign a release stating that the warden and other staff had permission to open, read, and inspect his mail. A majority of the prisons did not allow the inmate to make telephone calls or limited them to family emergencies. About half the institutions restricted the number of outside visitors to one a week or less, and most restricted visiting days. In the vast majority of cases, the reason for restricting contact with the outside was security and/or administrative convenience. Such policies make it evident that the Quaker conception of the penitentiary has been stood on its head. Instead of the staff trying to restrict mutually corrosive contact between inmates as the Quakers had advocated, the staff spend their time restricting contact between the inmate and the outside world.

The hostility towards visitors is ultimately self-defeating to the correctional system. One cannot deny the public access to institutions because inmates are dangerous and then expect them to receive discharged inmates in their midst. One cannot rigidly control the flow of information out of the institutions, through direct mail censorship and prohibitions against staff discussing prison policies, and then complain about prisons getting a bad press. Whatever press coverage the prison system has received over the past century has been almost entirely controlled by the prison authorities themselves. Instead of realistic accounts of prison life in the media, we hear only about stabbings and assaults or we see on TV a romanticized version of The Big House. We have taken the opposite direction from the pre-penitentiary practice of making an example of offenders through public ridicule. Instead we hide them in remote places out of public view and then romanticize them. The biased flow of information about imprisonment in the media has important implications for those who would like to change the present system. One cannot assume that the public is adequately informed about prison issues. Indeed one must assume that the public is badly informed. This is a serious indictment of those people in the criminal justice system whose duties consist of regulating the flow of information to the outside.

Many of the problems connected with imprisonment are related to its hidden secretive aspects. The convicted person is removed from the community and placed out of sight. The fact that he or she is hidden from public scrutiny increases the likelihood of abuse to the point of inevitability. Put one group of men under the absolute domination of another group of men for a long period of time *outside public view,* and there will be numerous abuses. One can try to select saints to be the keepers, but the result will be the same. If the situation of dominance/subordination is kept within the public view, however, the likelihood of abuses will be reduced. Opening up prisons is not the ultimate reform but it is a step forwards.

Public Trial, Private Punishment

The courts today are under similar pressure to stop crime, yet they have retained a higher degree of legitimacy than the penal system. This is partly due to the legal requirement of public access. The accused has the right to a public trial but not a public punishment. Jurists regard public access as a necessary ingredient of a trial. There is a real abhorrence of secret trials. Even though the onlookers play no formal role in the deliberations, as they might do in a People's Court in Cuba, they provide a backdrop of legitimacy to the proceedings. The main objectives of making trials public are protection of the defendant's rights and education of the community. However, particularly in celebrated cases, the pre-trial investigation and the trial itself have also acquired many of the aspects of punishment. By the time a defendant has spent six to eight months in the media spotlight during the pretrial maneuvering and jury selection, and then undergone a lengthy trial, followed by an appeals period if he is convicted, it is logical for a judge to conclude that he has suffered enough and release him. The time and expense of all this activity and the tarnishing of reputations exceed what most people believe to be fair punishment. After years of investigations, trials, and appeals, the imprisonment of a celebrated defendant is an anti-climax. One of the reporters covering the Attica trial, which took place more than four years after the 1971 disturbance, declared: "It's as if we were paleontologists looking at the bones of some ancient event." [5] The main figures of the trial appeared to be not the defendants but the two defense lawyers, William Kunstler and former attorney general Ramsey Clark. There are strong feelings in America against public humiliation. Compared to the objective harshness of other penalties imposed, these feelings are practically in the realm of paleologic. Gary Wardrip was arrested for flag desecration when he used an American flag to partition the rear of his minibus. After he pleaded guilty, the twenty-one-year-old assembly line worker found that he faced the possibility of a $1000 fine. As an alternative, the judge insisted that Wardrip stand outside the city hall holding a flag for three hours. A crowd of townspeople gathered for his public penance. "It was like the old days when they slapped you in the stocks," Wardrip reported. After an hour he could take no more and pleaded with the judge, "I don't care what happens, I can't face the people outside." The judge declared that the intent of the sentence was "embarrassment" but relented and permitted Wardrip to finish the three hours holding the flag in a closed courtroom. "It tore me down—and my family," declared Wardrip, who explained that he had left the flag hanging in his bus "to show his patriotism" and insisted that he really liked the American flag. A reporter covering the incident took umbrage at the novel sentence and asked rhetorically whether or not the use of the flag as a partition was a greater desecration than using it as a means of embarrassing a U.S. citizen.[6]

My colleague Humphry Osmond, a psychiatrist by trade, pondered the incident.[7] He could not understand why the young man would not be willing to spend three hours holding the flag, which he said he really liked, to save a $1000 fine. The sentence obviously had a strong deterrent effect on Wardrip, who is not about to repeat his offense, and on the citizens of his community, who observed his public penance. The novel sentence saved the citizens the cost of incarcerating Wardrip and the corrosive effect of the jail environment on a first offender.

Cases such as this support the observation that Americans are more moved by shame than by guilt. Having others know that one has done something wrong is more difficult to bear than knowing it oneself. A thousand-dollar fine or sixty days in jail, while onerous, can be undergone in private. Indeed, the essence of imprisonment is removal from public view. This neglected component of imprisonment is one of the strongest reasons for its popularity in American society. A substantial fine or penalty administered in private is much easier to bear than a lesser penalty in public. It seems likely that this wish for privacy lies behind the frequent use of plea bargaining to avoid a public trial. However, the secrecy of plea bargaining arrangements makes them susceptible to manipulation by those with power and influence.

Between 75 and 90 per cent of all felony convictions are obtained as a result of plea bargaining. Contrary to the public view, this is not an illegal, underhanded practice that occurs only between shady lawyers and crooked prosecutors. Rather it is the ordinary, accepted method of handling offenders. As former police chief Patrick Murphy described it, a judge will "knock lawyers' heads together to reach a prompt settlement." As the courts operate today, plea bargaining is essential to the workings of the system. Murphy also describes a study in New York City where, in 1970, the police made 94,042 arrests for felonies but only 552 of these cases even came to trial.[8] This occurred at a time when the courts in New York City were complaining of a heavy workload. If the number of felony arrests coming to trial rose from 1 to 5 per cent of all felony arrests, the courts would have been swamped under a five-fold increase in workload! Murphy also analyzed 136 arrests for felonious possession of pistols in New York City in 1970. Not one of the 136 was convicted of the original charge. Eventually 53 went to prison for a little over an average of one month each. While the courts have been unwilling to consider long-term incarceration to be a cruel punishment, its discriminatory application may compel them to find it so unusual and the criteria so arbitrary as to make it unconstitutional.

A study of all homicide indictments in New York State in 1973 revealed the typical sequence of events.[9] First, a grand jury indicts the suspect for murder, the most serious homicide charge. But court backlogs and delays prevent a prompt trial, thus leading to out-of-court negotiations between the prosecutor and the defense, culminating in the defendant agreeing to change his plea of innocent to the original homicide charge to a plea of guilty on a less serious charge. By accepting the guilty plea the district attorney avoids the necessity of a trial, and the defendant is virtually guaranteed a lesser sentence than he would have received if he had been convicted by a jury. Faced with the bargain worked out between the prosecutor and the defense, the judge completes the process by granting the defendant—who had originally been charged with murder—immediate freedom on probation or a prison sentence of less than ten years. The major function of the pretrial maneuvering by both sides is to prevent a case from coming to trial. When and if a case actually comes to trial, it usually means that one side or the other wants to emphasize its educational and symbolic value. There is widespread public misunderstanding about plea bargaining which, if left uncorrected, will eventually erode confidence in the jury system.

Watergate Sentences

> I was glad when Hunt and company were released. Prison is evil. No human being should be there unless he has killed dispassionately or is a clear danger to the physical survival of others. I was ultimately more glad than galled when Spiro T. Agnew . . . walked.
>
> CLIFFORD IRVING

Most people agree that punishment was necessary for the Watergate conspirators. They had to be held accountable for their misdeeds as an affirmation of the viability of a government of laws and as an example to others who might contemplate similar misconduct. Furthermore, most of us agree that in their case reform is not the issue. There is no mention that Colson, Magruder, or Kalmbach were enrolled in vocational training, correspondence courses, or group therapy. They had strayed, but they knew the way back, and the function of punishment was to set them back on the correct path. At Allenwood and Lompoc they were housed with other prisoners who had committed offenses that were not of a violent or sexual nature. Many were middle-class narcotics offenders. According to Allenwood's Warden Taylor, Magruder was not an ostensible threat to society and lacked "criminal sophistication." Most prisons are likely to produce these very qualities, but not in Magruder's case, because the segregated prison system kept him from contact with those who had acquired that sophistication coming up through the ranks from juvenile hall and county jail. Note the difference between the treatment of Watergate inmates, for whom the prison sentence was primarily a retribution and a deterrent to others in public trust, and that meted out to a young car thief or burglar who needs to be reformed. The degree of confinement, dehumanization, and humiliation is directly related to the degree to which reform is required. Violent offenders are likely to be held under conditions of greatest security and least amenity. Those prisoners who are least compliant and most violently object to prison procedures end up in maximum-security institutions. It seems odd that those people for whom behavior change is most critical are subjected to far more punishing environments than those for whom our intention is clearly retribution.

Had the President's men been sent to more oppressive institutions, the pressures for prison reform would have increased. Yet it is difficult to suggest that these men, or any people, should be subjected to the worst aspects of the American penal system. Putting Charles Colson in a strip cell with no furniture except a steel cot and a hole in the floor for a toilet would quickly result in changes in the atmosphere of the Soledad Adjustment Center, but the Charles Colsons are sent not to Soledad, or even Leavenworth, but to Allenwood. Jimmy Hoffa and Mickey Cohen emerged from prison as vocal spokesmen for prison reform, but both men spent time in medium- or maximum-security institutions. Hoffa described the federal prison system as "so undisciplined and so ill-run that the imagination of man can't comprehend what goes on." Alfred Hassler, a conscientious objector confined in Lewisburg, concluded that "the best of prisons does not reform or rehabilitate. . . . Time is wasted, useless, the bitterness inflicted on inmates by the reasonless, unaware, impersonal monster outside called society."[10] Hassler spent much of his time trying to persuade the humane guards he found to leave prison work before they became brutalized. Philip Berrigan left prison predicting that more Atticas were inevitable.

The presence of so many prominent inmates is one reason why Lompoc and Allenwood remain showcase institutions. The fear of adverse publicity if anything should happen to a celebrated inmate is a strong deterrent to any guard or administrator who might want to practice the brutality commonplace in maximum-security institutions. For the inmates in Allenwood and Lompoc, the main problem is boredom. This would be a great advance for those inmates presently confined in other state and federal institutions, whose immediate goal is to make these oppressive places more like Allenwood and Lompoc. Yet the wasted months of Magruder, Kalmbach, et al. raise questions as to the value of confinement even under humane conditions. Apart from those administrators and suppliers in the prison business, nobody gains when these men are taken from their families and housed and fed at the taxpayers' expense. It would seem far more logical to sentence Charles Colson to two years of putting his legal training in the service of the poor of Appalachia than to send him off to play golf and convert his former colleagues to his new-found religion. John Ehrlichman, a land-use lawyer before becoming the President's chief adviser on domestic policies, formally requested alternative service. Ehrlichman had spent part of the two months between his conviction and his sentencing looking for a place where his legal experience could be put to use in the public interest. His lawyer formally requested a "strict sentence . . . to do penance with good deeds"—helping Indian tribes in northern New Mexico establish tribal boundaries and property rights. It would undoubtedly be cheaper to find tennis courts closer to Magruder's home and sentence him to spend a prescribed number of hours there each day than to keep him in Allenwood. Despite the amenities, no one is going to confuse Allenwood with paradise. There is a lot of room for improvement, particularly in meeting privacy needs and in dealing with the problems created by an exclusively male society. The federal prison at Fort Worth and the Massachusetts State Prison at Framingham are already co-ed, and other institutions are considering this innovation. Although this is a step forwards, society must stop creating expensive institutional substitutes for things that already exist in the community. Rather than attempt to find Magruder a surrogate sex partner, how much more logical it would be to leave Magruder with his wife and children as their breadwinner and companion. The experience of the Watergate inmates illustrates how meaningless and irrelevant incarceration at a showcase institution can be. If these places provide nothing beneficial to inmates or society, the lesson must be clearly drawn that the way to go is not in the direction of more modern institutions with golf courses and tennis courts. Instead, money should go into the pilot programs and alternatives to incarceration. We can be grateful to the President's men for showing us that the best the federal correctional system can offer isn't good enough.

When Judge John Sirica ordered the Watergate figures still in jail to be released on January 8, 1975, he announced that they had suffered enough. This suggests that he was using a retribution model. Society had in his opinion already exacted its pound of flesh. This was also the argument used by those who supported the pardon of former President Nixon by his successor. Defenders of the pardon maintain that the disgrace in being forced to resign from office was sufficient punishment. It seems noteworthy that in Nixon's case there were loud cries throughout the nation for further punishment, while very few were raised in response to the release of those Watergate figures who had actually served time in jail. One reason is that Magruder, Dean, and Kalmbach had been behind bars, while the former President had not. Another important difference is that the men released early admitted their guilt and cooperated with the prosecution. Their repentance (public confession) and restitution (cooperation with the prosecution) made their early release more palatable to the public. It seems likely, however, that social disgrace will be accepted by the public as legitimate only in the case of a well-known public figure. The plea of a gas station attendant convicted of burglary that he should not be sent to jail because he has already suffered enough would probably not be accepted by most judges even though the defendant might be shunned in his own social circle.

The conviction of a prominent person increases his or her market value on the lecture circuit and as a potential author. John Dean received an average of $3500 per lecture on his lecture tour of campuses. Even such a minor Watergate figure as Donald Segretti received $1200 for a talk at Missouri Western State College. Former President Nixon was reported to have sold his autobiography for $2 million, and Magruder's book made the best-seller list, with earnings reported close to $250,000. Both Hunt and Colson reportedly received advances in six figures for their books. There has been ample precedent for such payments. Television networks gave lavish fees to such non-Watergate figures as Sirhan Sirhan (NBC) and William Calley (ABC), and most recently Watergate figures G. Gordon Liddy and H. R. Haldeman were paid $15,000 and $50,000 respectively for television appearances. One wonders how such payments can be reconciled with a deterrent model. Perhaps if judges were more perceptive about the financial returns of notoriety, remunerative public confession could be inserted into a restitution model. The offender could be sentenced to return 75 per cent of all financial gain accruing from his notoriety to a specified charity. The idea that a prominent person has suffered enough because of public exposure must be balanced by the cash value of notoriety; the notion of someone receiving $4000 for a one-hour talk is somewhat amazing.

It seems obvious that the Watergate men were an undistinguished lot; there were no heroes among them. They were rather ordinary people too close to the temptations of immense power. Reducing Watergate to the personalities of the individuals involved is an example of idealistic thinking, out of which comes the desire to "get rid of the bad apples" without much attention to the conditions producing the rot and decay. I don't begrudge the Watergaters their lecture and book fees. In this society everyone needs a hustle, and for those who have been disgraced, disbarred, or stigmatized the need is much greater. Their days on the lucrative lecture circuit are limited. The media spotlight doesn't stay in one place very long; in a short while they will be reduced to the small-town evangelical circuit.

Myth of Rehabilitation

With the Watergate conspirators, prison officials could not employ euphemisms about any kind of rehabilitation. It is no acccdent that it was during this time that a U.S. attorney general declared that rehabilitation was a myth. Jail, according to then-Attorney General William Saxbe, is for punishment, not reform.[11] Public officials across the country gratefully seized upon the opportunity to extricate themselves from the model muddle in which they had been mired. California's director of corrections declared, "Prison is for people society can't stomach. Don't kid yourself about rehabilitation." A spokesman for the Federal Bureau of Prison announced that the bureau was "backing away from rehabilitation by changing the terms it is using and by dropping the requirement that all prisoners must choose some educational or vocational program to pursue while in prison." [12] This is frank talk in a field renowned for its reliance on sugar-coating and obfuscation. The only real surprise is that these admissions were made for public consumption.

In place of rehabilitation, Saxbe would like to substitute two other goals for the prison—deterrence and confession. "First," he believes, "you have to make a criminal realize that there is a definite penalty for a violation of the law." This will show him that he is a "loser" and reduce the "prestige from outsmarting the law and being clever." This makes sense for the Watergate inmates, who enjoyed prominent positions, but not for most ordinary criminals, who already know that they are losers. Their demeaned status has been brought home to them in an unending series of unhappy encounters with school authorities, police, courts, juvenile halls, etc. Second, Saxbe wants the criminal to admit guilt. Interestingly, confession happens to be a mainstay of the judicial system in the Soviet Union and China, although they use it as a goal of the trial rather than of imprisonment. A black marketeer recently convicted in China was released as soon as he publicly confessed the error of his ways. However, the American court system provides no incentive for a person charged to make a public confession, except as a plea bargain on a lesser offense. A person will be encouraged to inform on others, casting the net of guilt still wider, but all the practical considerations discourage public acknowledgment of guilt prior to conviction. However, the situation changes once a person is incarcerated. Parole boards look upon the admission of guilt as a significant index of reform. The inmate who had previously been advised to keep silent and admit only the most minimal transgression must now learn to publicly acknowledge his wrongdoing. This is inconsistent with all that has gone on before. Confession makes no sense as a goal of confinement in an institution dominated by criminal values.

The acknowledgment that rehabilitation is a myth undermines the legitimacy of the indeterminate sentence law. Parole boards look for "proof of rehabilitation" before they will release inmates sentenced for an indefinite period. Typically an inmate demonstrates his rehabilitation by enrolling in school courses, attending AA meetings, and staying out of trouble. Everyone recognizes that institutional adjustment has no inherent connection with adjustment outside, but if the very notion of rehabilitation inside prison is itself false, the parole boards are looking for a chimera. It is no wonder that sentences served under California's indeterminate sentence law have been 92 per cent longer than sentences elsewhere in the nation, and 72 per cent longer than sentences in other industrial states such as New York and Illinois. Parole boards are looking for the rehabilitation that the attorney general and other officials claim does not exist, except perhaps among first offenders and the young.

Courts are now being asked to decide whether or not an inmate has the right *not* to be rehabilitated. The Constitution does not grant anyone the right to remain exactly as he is, but there are some constitutional protections in the Fourth Amendment against unreasonable search and seizures and in the Fifth Amendment against self-incrimination, and the Eighth Amendment's proscription of cruel and unusual punishment. Any court passing upon the right not to be rehabilitated is going to find itself mired so deeply in the model muddle that it will never come out with any semblance of logic. What does it mean for an inmate to maintain a right *not to return to a former state in which he got in trouble with the law?* Such sophistry ill befits so serious a matter as a deprivation of liberty.

Many judges unfamiliar with the program limitations of prisons still announce to the person being sentenced that they are sending him to prison "to be rehabilitated." Richard McGee, former director of the Washington and the California prison systems, maintains that this is as irrational as sending an offender to prison to have his appendix removed or to learn the trade of his choice.[13] The state has the responsibility of providing rehabilitation opportunities to a person deprived of liberty, just as it has an obligation to feed him and provide him with necessary medical care. It is important to distinguish between the reason for sending a convicted person to prison and the state's obligation to do something for him after he gets there. Rehabilitation, McGee believes, does work for some offenders and should be a principal objective of correctional programs, *but should not be the reason for the imposition of a sentence.*

Background Note

A number of high government officials involved in the Watergate burglary, coverup, or related incidents pleaded guilty or were found guilty by the courts. Some went to jail and some did not. The following individuals were mentioned in this chapter:

John Dean, former counsel to President Nixon, later served as the government's chief witness. He pleaded guilty to conspiracy to obstruct justice and defraud the United States and was sentenced to one to four years in prison. Dean was released by Judge Sirica after serving four months.

Jeb Magruder, a key figure in President Nixon's re-election committee, pleaded guilty of conspiracy to obstruct justice and defraud the United States. He was sentenced to ten to forty-eight months in prison and served seven months in Allenwood before being released.

Herbert Kalmbach, President Nixon's lawyer, pleaded guilty to one felony act charging violations of the Federal Corrupt Practices Act and another misdemeanor charge. He received a six-to-eighteen-months' sentence and a $10,000 fine. He served six months in the Lompoc Federal Prison before being released by Judge Sirica.

Egil Krogh, who held various federal positions, pleaded guilty to complicity in the burglary of a psychiatrist's office and served six months in Allenwood.

Charles Colson, a close adviser to the President, pleaded guilty to obstructing justice and was sentenced to one to three years. He was released by a federal judge on humanitarian grounds after serving seven months.

John D. Ehrlichman, the President's chief adviser for domestic affairs, was sentenced to two and a half to eight years in prison for covering up the Watergate scandal. He had previously been sentenced along with Krogh for his part in an earlier Watergate-related burglary. At the present time, both sentences are under appeal.

THE BEHAVIOR MOD SCARE 8

It is inconceivable to me that prisoners like Charlie Manson and his followers will be released into the streets without any attempt to modify their behavior. If the modification of their criminal behavior means employing aversive stimuli, so what? The world outside prison walls deserves some assurance that what takes place within prison walls is affecting change in prisoner behavior.

Letter-to-the-Editor, *Human Behavior* magazine

Washington—the government has banned any further use of federal anti-crime funds for behavior modification, calling a halt to the program they had conducted in the name of law enforcement for the systematic manipulation of the behavior of inmates, juvenile offenders, and alcoholics. *N.Y. Times* News Service, February 15, 1975.

Behavior modification has been getting a bad press. This is nothing new in a field whose major figures—Pavlov, Watson, and Skinner—have long been regarded as mechanistic, simplistic, and inhumane. Films such as *A Clockwork Orange* and *The Manchurian Candidate* showed a wide audience how a totalitarian state can maintain its control through behavior conditioning. Unfortunately, the most recent controversy has not occurred in the cinema, but in prison. Jessica Mitford has provided a valuable and necessary overview on the relationship between drug companies, the federal government, universities, and prisons.[1] She documented the way that prisoners have been subsidizing pharmaceutical companies in countless experiments with untried drugs and other medical procedures. Inmates are more accessible for the drug companies and cheaper, and there is less risk of a lawsuit than with outside volunteers. Several courts have recently ruled that "informed consent" has little meaning in an institution where all aspects of life are under the total control of the authorities. Many prisoners frankly admit that they volunteer for medical experiments because it will look good on their record or because they are told to do so. At a nearby state prison, the second largest source of inmate income is participation in medical experimentation. Mitford's book put together many isolated incidents of institutional brutality under the guise of research and showed that these were part of a general pattern of inmate exploitation for the benefit of the medical industry. I will not repeat the grisly tales of what Wayne Sage has called the Clockwork Lemon approach—lemon rather than orange because the techniques were generally unsuccessful as well as brutal.[2] The horror stories of psychosurgery on prisoners, both with and without consent, and of drug-induced fear have been told sufficiently often and are readily available elsewhere. If the medical atrocities were all there were to behavior modification, it would not require another chapter. However, behavior modification has become one of those scare terms whose original meaning has been infused with paleologic. Most recently it has been used in the press as synonymous with any punitive procedure. This is an inaccurate characterization of a field with respectable traditions in scientific psychology. Behaviorism, the philosophy underlying behavior mod, produced a coherent theory of motivation, whose techniques and hardware have been applied successfully in school and industry, and which, according to many authorities, has wide application in corrections.

A close look at behavior modification will show how two innocuous words can suddenly become a scare term, producing an immediate recourse to euphemism (keep the methods but find a new name); a model muddle (change the inmates versus leave their heads alone); and a tendency to scapegoat (the white-coated doctor or the inmate himself). Behavior modification is new enough in corrections to let us see how it got in, what it has done, and how it has been abused. We will begin with a brief history of the origins of behaviorism, the general field whose application to the realm of human affairs is variously called behavior modification or behavior therapy. Then we will briefly discuss how behavior mod has been applied in institutions for the retarded, the insane, and the criminal offender. The history of behavior modification reveals why it has found such fertile soil in institutions where all aspects of the inmate's life are under the control of the staff. Finally, we will attempt an overview on the problems and potential of behavior modification, both in and out of the prison.

Origins

Unlike psychoanalysis and other forms of talk therapy which originated in the clinic, behaviorism began in the laboratory, and the subjects were animals rather than people. The Russian physiologist I. M. Pavlov and his students demonstrated that it was possible to establish an association between a stimulus and a previously unrelated response, such as a bell and salivation, which Pavlov called a *conditioned reflex.*[3] Such connections could be objectively created using rigorous laboratory procedures, without considering subjective phenomena such as ideas, attitudes, or motives. By changing the order in which things were presented, or altering the timing between stimulus and reward, the animal could be conditioned according to the experimenter's plan. This procedure, in which the organism is relatively passive while an association is formed between two items occurring together, is today termed *classical conditioning.* A dog in Pavlov's lab would be harnessed in his cage so that his saliva could be measured as the sound of a bell became associated with the appearance of meat powder. Pavlov believed such conditioned reflexes to be the building blocks of learning. In America, psychologist John B. Watson developed this research into a behavioristic theory intended to fit people as well as animals. Watson's early work in artificially inducing a fear response illustrates the ethical dilemmas behavior modification was later to face.[4] By combining the presence of a white rat with a loud unpleasant noise, Watson and Rayner made a young boy named Albert fearful of the rat, and subsequently of anything white and fuzzy, including a woman's fur coat and a man with a white beard. No one seems to know whether or not Albert went through life afraid of white furry things.

B. F. Skinner subsequently developed another type of learning procedure which he termed *operant conditioning*.[5] Skinner found that an animal would act in such a way as to maximize rewards such as food. By arranging its environment so that reinforcement was given for certain actions and not for others, the researcher could shape the animal's behavior. If a rat received food pellets every time it pushed a lever, it would press the lever when hungry. These simple methods of "shaping behavior" could be extended to more complex behaviors by linking together several conditioning procedures. Keller and Marion Breland, two students of Skinner's, used these methods to train animals for public exhibitions and county fairs.[6] "Casey at the Bat" involved a chicken playing baseball on a small diamond. When a small ball came down the strike zone, the chicken would peck a button to activate a bat. If the bat happened to hit the ball into the fair zone, the chicken would run to first base. By linking together a number of conditioned responses, the Brelands had presumably taught Casey the rudiments of baseball. Today this research is highly mechanized, and the responses of animals in sealed cages are registered on tape fed into a computer and printed out almost immediately.

The origin of this work in the animal laboratory is significant for several reasons. In the animal laboratory ethical problems are less than in human society, and control over the environment is readily obtained. Such advantages in doing experimental research become liabilities when it comes time to apply these findings in the world of people. There is little in the animal laboratory that prepares an investigator for the ethical requirements for informed voluntary consent in human experimentation. There is the real risk that the experimenter who has been reinforced for playing God in the laboratory will carry over that attitude into work with people.

Ogden Lindsley was one of the first to apply Skinner's method in an institutional setting.[7] Lindsley found that hospitalized schizophrenic patients would perform simple laboratory tasks, such as pressing levers in response to lights or buzzers, in order to obtain candy, cigarettes, or other reinforcers. Lindsley is generally credited with first using the term *behavior therapy*. This term remained common in English clinical psychology, but in the United States such techniques were known as *behavior modification* up until the recent controversy. Because of the inherent ambiguity of the phrase *behavior modification,* in that any attempt to change behavior, whether by psychoanalysis, encounter groups, or drugs, has as its objective the modifying of behavior, there is a movement today to return to the older term *behavior therapy*. This seems preferable to some of the euphemisms currently being proposed, such as that put forward by Leonard Krasner, chairman of the Commission of Behavioral Modification of the American Psychological Association, who would like to substitute the term *environmental design* for behavior modification.[8] Eysenck defines behavior therapy as "the attempt to alter human behavior and emotion in a beneficial manner according to the laws of modern learning theory." [9] In a brief review of behavior therapy, Ramsay included four different techniques: desensitization to anxiety-provoking stimuli; assertiveness training designed to strengthen social responses; aversion therapy designed to associate nonadaptive behaviors with unpleasant experiences; and operant conditioning aimed at restructuring the environment to reinforce desirable behaviors.[10]

The early research by Lindsley demonstrated that relatively simple conditioning procedures could be used successfully with chronic mental patients. However, the classes of responses that were conditioned were not very significant. The task of extending these procedures to meaningful social situations fell to other investigators, such as Teodoro Ayllon and Nathan Azrin,[11] Harold Cohen,[12] and Montrose Wolf,[13] working in mental hospitals, schools for retarded, reformatories for juveniles, and state prisons. The first systematic application of operant conditioning using an entire hospital ward as a social system took place in Weyburn, Canada, in 1958. Teodoro Ayllon was put in charge of a ward of chronic mental patients who had been assigned to him because of their specific behavioral problems.[14] His methods were frequently opposite to those which had been used under the previous Freudian approach. Prior to Ayllon's coming, when a certain patient went to the nurses talking about her nonexistent physical complaints, the nurses would try to console her, talk to her in order to find out what was ailing her, and then try to persuade her that her fears were groundless. Unfortunately, the delusions of schizophrenic patients are remarkably resistant to this kind of persuasion. Ayllon reasoned that the nurses were actually reinforcing the patient's delusions. Instead, he instructed the nurses to "look away and act busy" when the patient talked about nonexistent complaints. Incidentally, a thorough medical examination had demonstrated that the complaints were indeed groundless. When this patient talked to the nurses about anything else, such as the weather, a visit outside, or any ward event, the nurses paid a great deal of attention to her, gave her coffee, brought her to the canteen, and otherwise reinforced this behavior. Under the new regime the patient rather quickly switched from talking about her imagined bodily illnesses to talking about other things. The same methods of extinguishing undesirable behaviors and rewarding desired behaviors were successfully applied to patients who were overweight, who hoarded towels, who sat on the floor, and who bothered the nurses with unreasonable requests. Later, Ayllon joined Nathan Azrin at Anna State Hospital in Illinois and developed the first ward based upon a *token economy*.[15] Here, the investigators broke dramatically with the origins of their research in the animal laboratory to take advantage of the symbolic capacity of humans. Rather than allowing the research subjects to find out the desired behaviors only through trial and error, Ayllon and Azrin posted a list of desired behaviors on the wall and then gave bonus points (tokens) to those patients who made their beds, swept their rooms, worked in the kitchen, etc. These tokens were redeemable for canteen items or for amenities such as a color TV, staying up later at night, or a private room. These incentives proved very effective in motivating the patients to look after themselves and take care of the ward.

More relevant for our purposes is the work of Harold Cohen, who developed a token economy in a school for delinquent boys.[16] In the typical school system, reinforcement is vague, inconsistent, and often omitted entirely in favor of punishment for failure. The student who does something right is permitted to continue, but the student who does something wrong is ridiculed and thereby given extra attention. Cohen made the rewards system explicit by telling the boys exactly what they had to do to earn their tokens, which were given promptly for desired behaviors. Cohen demonstrated that academic achievement, among other things, could be raised substantially when tangible rewards were given on an explicit basis. At the Draper Correctional Center in Alabama, John McKee used a token economy to motivate adult felons towards academic achievement and routine institutional tasks.[17] Psychologist Scott Geller organized a four-stage token economy program to be used as a model for the maximum-security prison at Mecklenburg, Virginia.[18] The aim of the program, which was funded by the Department of Justice, was to modify the behavior of troublesome inmates using small rewards—Cokes, candy bars, typing lessons, or televison viewing—which inmates could earn by keeping their cells neat, taking part in prison activities, and improving their educational skills. The inmates were to be evaluated daily by project staff members, mostly students with bachelor's degrees in psychology, who would enter the earned credits on wallet-sized plastic credit cards which later could be redeemed for commissary items. Participation in the program was intended to be completely voluntary. An inmate could drop out at any time without reprisal. Stages 1 and 2 were conducted in the maximum-security cells of the state penitentiary; the inmates who progressed to Stages 3 and 4 were to be transferred to a lower-security prison where they would have more freedom of movement and earn actual money, rather than plastic points, for work in data processing.

From Use to Abuse

Would that the history of behavior modification could end on this hopeful note! We could say that behavior modification represents a proven method for motivating inmates to engage in socially desirable behavior. Unfortunately the nature of the American prison makes such a conclusion unwarranted. What happened to behavior modification illustrates the reasons why imprisonment itself must be ended. Any situation in which large numbers of people are deprived of their liberty for long periods, have no rights but only privileges, and are removed from society and hidden from public view, is fraught with possibilities for abuse; and some of this did occur in the name of behavior modification. It can be demonstrated that the problem was not with the methods of behavior modification, but with the prison itself. In a totalitarian setting, any technique for behavior change, whether it is psychoanalysis, drug therapy, or encounter groups, is likely to become an agent of oppression.

In an earlier chapter I committed myself to avoiding the litany of horror stories of confinement. These are so well known and well documented that they don't need repeating. When it comes to behavior modification, I have to qualify my original intention in order to demonstrate that certain techniques really aren't behavior modification in the technical sense of the phrase. I refer specifically to psychosurgery and the use of psychoactive drugs. However, some of the brutal research undertaken in prisons, most of it now discontinued, does bear an embarrassingly close resemblance to the procedures developed by Pavlov and Skinner. Several inmates at Vacaville (California) prison were given anectine, a curare-like drug which made the inmate feel as if he had lost control over his breathing and was going to die. The researcher's goal was to use classical conditioning to link together this terrible fear response and imprisonment. Elsewhere, the defunct START Program at the federal prison in Springfield, Missouri, illustrated the hazards of an unethical application of operant conditioning. At the onset of the special program, inmates were stripped of their customary rights and amenities. Each prisoner began the program in solitary confinement and had to win back his freedom by demonstrating a more positive attitude, which meant following the rules more closely. After the threat of several lawsuits, the Federal Bureau of Prisons announced that it was closing down the program for "economic reasons" and for low enrollment. Attorney Arpier Saunders of the National Prison Project, who represented inmates in their suit against START, maintained that "the START suit is not intended to stamp out all behavior mod programs in prisons, but I think there is a real legal and ethical question whether behaviorists can apply clinical methods to involuntary subjects." The president of the American Psychological Association at the time, Albert Bandura, admitted that in too many institutions these programs are designed to keep the institutions running smoothly rather than to help the inmates. Regardless of original intentions, they become merely "management devices." [19] The associate director of Maryland's Patuxent Institute, psychologist Arthur Kandel, described the segregation cells, known to inmates as The Hole, as "negative reinforcers . . . used as positive treatment conditions." [20] The courts later ruled that lengthy confinement in these cells constituted cruel and unusual punishment. An article in *Science* declared, "Any activities in the penal system that go under the name 'research' are regarded with suspicion by civil libertarians, and with downright fear by the increasing number of prisoners who see themselves as victims of political and racist oppression." [21] Civil liberties groups have also criticized token economies and other approaches to behavior modification even when they have not employed aversive conditioning. Token rewards are seen as merely that—tokens. Instead of working for canteen privileges or a better cell assignment, inmates demand to be paid the prevailing wage for working in the kitchen, laundry, or tag plant.

Balance Sheet

This brief historical review should provide some understanding of why behavior mod found such a receptive climate in total institutions. However, it is patently unfair to blame B. F. Skinner for the Clockwork Lemon. Skinner has vociferously maintained that reward is most effective in inducing learning, and that extinction (non-reward) is preferable to punishment in eliminating unwanted responses. In no way did he sanction, or would he have sanctioned, the drug and surgery experiments carried out at Vacaville. Physical treatments such as psychosurgery, hormone treatment, or drug therapy are completely antithetical to the logic and practice of behavior modification. In most of the institutions where token economies have been used, the use of drugs and physical treatments has decreased because, in the experimenter's eyes, tranquilizing drugs will inhibit conditioning. This is not to imply that all behaviorists are opposed to drugs, but only that drugs are not essential or even desirable in a behavior modification program. As for psychosurgery or any other procedure in which portions of the brain are cut away, these are contrary to the behaviorist's "black box" approach to the human organism. The behaviorist is probably less interested than any other type of psychologist in tinkering with the insides of the human brain. Paradoxically, it is the humanistic psychologists who are so enamored of alpha-wave conditioning and other biofeedback procedures, as well as of drugs as a means of altering states of consciousness. When it comes to drugs and biofeedback, the behaviorist seems downright anti-biological. The Prisoners Union, which maintains that it doesn't want anyone messing around inside the inmate's head, would find strong support among the followers of Skinner. The true behaviorist doesn't want to brainwash anyone; all he wants to do is change *behavior*. If offenders will cease violating the law and mental patients will stop acting crazy, that is sufficient.

Whether or not their thoughts are pure or coherent is beside the point. The identification of behavior modification with "brainwashing" is based on the lumping together of unrelated techniques and theories.

Most token economies today eschew aversive procedures completely in favor of positive incentives. The behavior modifier claims that he or she is doing on a systematic basis (granting rewards for good behavior) what was done haphazardly and unsystematically before. In the typical prison, rewards (extra privileges or early release) are bestowed by the staff capriciously. Privileges promised by one guard are denied by another. Everything is vague and inexplicit—*maybe* if the inmate behaves properly, he will be transferred to another unit, or *maybe* he will get a better job, or *maybe* he will be given a furlough home. A token economy makes all these transactions explicit and contingent upon certain specified behavior on the part of the inmate. Rather than telling the inmate that *maybe* he'll earn a visit home, he is told explicitly that he will be given a visit home *when* he does certain specified things. Any attempt by the administration to establish unethical or immoral transactions would quickly be exposed, since everything is explicit. Ideally, an inmate is able to insist upon a written statement of rewards and expected behaviors. According to the behaviorist, this should eliminate vague and unconstitutional staff contingencies regarding "political agitation" or "being a troublemaker," otherwise undefined.

Another criticism of behavior modification in prison is that its proponents know little about the history, organization, or record of the American penal system. ACLU lawyer Arpier Saunders criticizes "behavioral scientists getting into something they know nothing about, trying to apply textbook knowledge to a situation and a people they don't understand." [22] Saunders believes that the fundamental rule in prisons is that *anything that can be abused will be abused*. The good will of investigators and the best intentions of prison management will be unable to prevent abuse. Researchers generally have no operational control over inmates, who can be transferred elsewhere; wardens come and go; and the prison is hidden from public scrutiny. The isolation of the prison and the attitude that inmates have privileges rather than rights leaves any behavior change program open to severe abuse. The concept of outside review which is required of most research supported by the federal government is difficult to achieve in a closed society.

The fate of the token economy designed for Mecklenburg State Prison, described earlier, is illustrative. This project never got past the first two stages in the maximum-security prison. It was simultaneously attacked as too permissive by custodial staff and too manipulative by prisoners and civil liberties groups. The ACLU charged that the goal of the program was simply to make prisoners more docile and demanded a withdrawal of federal funds. In response to the criticism and the lax security in the minimum-security facility where vocational training was available, state officials canceled the later stages, withdrew the federal grant application, fired the psychologists, and developed their own stripped-down version of the program to modify the behavior of inmates who "disrupt institutional routine by venting aggression, cowering, or simply refusing to obey rules and regulations." The state official who had supported the program most vigorously was also fired. Psychologist Geller, who had directed the project from its inception, unhappily admitted, "We've been forced out of the picture. We are no longer supervising things. We have no idea of what they are doing." [23]

Most criticism of behavior modification has been directed toward the techniques rather than the ends. The Clockwork Lemon and Strangelove analogies dwell morbidly upon the methods used, the hardware, and the kinds of people who would apply this kind of power. This is a situation familiar to the student of criminal justice, who has seen most attention from the press, the public, and the courts directed to the techniques and hardware of punishment rather than its goals, seeking scapegoats for past mistakes rather than future results. The model muddle makes it extremely unlikely that any consensus will exist as to which behaviors should be conditioned and in which direction. In the absence of consensual long-range goals, short-run institutional goals will predominate. The behaviorist learns from his employer that his role is to change the inmate's behavior in a socially desirable direction, which usually means conformity with an institutional routine. White middle-class psychologists will be setting the adjustment criteria for predominantly poor and uneducated minority inmates. With a few significant exceptions, such as the psychosurgery and anectine studies, the ethical issues are connected less with the techniques or hardware than with the involuntary nature of the inmate's participation. I will describe two behavior modification programs, each employing Pavlovian conditioning procedures strong enough to turn the stomach; one does not meet the canons of professional ethics but the other does. These two examples should help clarify the ethical dilemmas involved in any application of behavior modification in prison.

Case A. Psychologists at the Somers, Connecticut, maximum-security prison apply electric shock in classical conditioning with convicted child molesters. During the twelve-week course, each inmate received small electric shocks on his inner thigh whenever a slide of a naked child is flashed on the screen, but no shock when a picture of an adult is shown. The shock is administered by a little black box that uses batteries to produce a current of half a milliampere at 100 volts. "It's really very low and doesn't hurt," declared the prison psychologist who administers the shocks. "It's so low that we don't dare tell the inmates how low it really is." In addition to the shocks, the inmates are put under hypnosis and taught to associate feared objects—such as heights, insects, or anything else they dislike—with thoughts of children. At the same time they are instructed to associate pleasant experiences with thoughts of adults.[24]

Case B. A Seattle-based firm, Health Research, Inc., offers a shock treatment program for people who want to stop smoking. The shocks are given by electrodes pressed to the forearm of the "patient," who is strapped to the electric machine in a small cubicle filled with stale, smelly cigarette butts and specimens of lungs rotting with emphysema. An unmerciful technician sends slight electric shocks (more nerve-racking than painful) through a smoker's arm each time he or she takes a puff. This aversion therapy is supplemented by group therapy during the five-day program, which costs $100.[25]

Looking at these two programs side by side, we find little to distinguish between them in goals or methods. Each illustrates the use of aversive conditioning to eliminate undesirable behavior. Both programs claim similar rates of cure, although the figures are still somewhat tentative. The program for sex offenders claims that nine out of fifteen repeated offenders have already been paroled and at least temporarily cured after completing the twelve-week course. The management of Health Research, Inc., states that 85 per cent of those completing the five-day conditioning program have not reverted to smoking. Neither success rate should be taken as accurate without some kind of outside verification. While the objectives, techniques, and even the reported success rates of the two programs are similar, one is under heavy fire from civil liberties groups and the other is not. The only difference between these two programs is that one involves prison inmates and the other voluntary patients who walk in off the streets, pay their $100, and can leave at any time. While the psychologists who run the Connecticut program assure the inmates of the voluntary nature of their participation and of their right to drop out of the program at any time, it is difficult to accept these assurances at face value in a prison setting. The psychologist running the program explained, "It's probably more voluntary than anything else that goes on in this place. We try very hard to make sure all our patients fully understand the program—it's one of the ways we select them." The director of the Connecticut branch of the ACLU, which voted to oppose the program, declared, "It's inherently coercive—there is no such thing as a real volunteer in a prison, especially when a prisoner knows that participating may enhance his chances for parole. If electric shock can be justified for 'volunteer' child molesters, why not for drug addicts, prostitutes, burglars, or 'habitual discipline problems'?" An ACLU inspection team discovered one behavior modification project in Missouri where the guards were put in charge and "the behavior mod became torture." [26]

Aversive conditioning is being used for a variety of behavioral problems on a voluntary outpatient basis in a fully ethical manner. The results, according to proponents of the programs, are as good or better than those obtained with other methods. The salient and unmistakable feature of these programs is that they are strictly voluntary. Amsterdam psychologist Ronald Ramsay uses aversive conditioning methods with adult homosexuals who want to change their own sexual preferences. This is done on a strictly voluntary basis with people whose attraction to their own sex causes them great mental suffering. Certainly this is not true of all homosexuals, but it is true of those patients who come to Ramsay for treatment. There is a clinic for alcoholics in Redwood City, California, employing the same sort of classical conditioning. Patients, all of whom are voluntary, first take emetine, which makes a person vomit if he later drinks alcohol. Even though he knows the consequences, each patient drinks alcohol, throws up, and then spends several hours in a small cubicle surrounded by open bottles of booze, half-full glasses of scotch and stale beer, and an open bucket containing his own vomit. The developers of the program claim a respectable record of cure for those who finish it.

At first hearing, the grisly details of these procedures fill the listener with horror. This is Strangelove, *1984,* and *Brave New World* brought together. Moral outrage is justified as a first reaction, but anyone dealing with problems as serious as alcoholism, child molesting, and nicotine addiction is required to go beyond a first impression. If *1984* and *Clockwork Orange* are abhorrent, so are *Lost Weekend, I'll Cry Tomorrow,* and *Skidrow Wino.* A fifty-year old man who has gone through three marriages, several careers, and tens of thousands of dollars in a twenty-year bout with alcoholism may be willing to subject himself to several weekends of aversive conditioning to overcome a long-established pattern of self-destruction. A participant in the aversive conditioning program for smokers mentioned above recalled that he had smoked three packs of cigarettes a day for twenty-six years. Then his doctor told him he had the first stages of emphysema, which led him to the program. "The doctor grabbed my cigarettes and said, 'This is your last pack, right?' " He tried to quit on his own, but failed. Fortunately the shock program was successful in getting him to give up his long-standing addiction. "It was an easy way to give up smoking. I don't even feel like lighting up—not even when my wife smokes in front of me—I don't think I ever will." It can be argued that he might have quit himself had he tried longer or harder, but this seems academic. He freely chose to pay his $100 and believes the program helped him.[27] Some conditioning programs sell people who finish the course a small self-shocking device which the person uses himself at the first signs of temptation in order to strengthen the associative bonds.

I am unwilling to fault these programs on their methods alone as long as participation is fully voluntary. They seem as defensible morally as the group therapy programs that rely on harsh words rather than electric shock. The drug addict who gets into a Synanon group can expect to have a mountain of abuse heaped upon him. He is told that he is a liar, a dope fiend, and a con artist who has been living a fake life. For many addicts, a small dose of electric shock would be far less punishing than this intense verbal abuse from people who claim that they know him better than he knows himself. Psychiatrist Martin Groder describes a Synanon game in the Marion, Ohio, Federal Penitentiary:

> Eight of them walked into the room and sat down—and I proceeded to rip them off, one after the other. I just shit all over them about all the things that had come to my attention that were so obvious to me about their trickiness, the lies, the misrepresentations, their attempts to get negative strokes by playing Kick Me, their inane dedication to stupidity, their tremendous fear of breaking any of the rules of the so-called "convict code" while at the same time being busily engaged in breaking them and covering up the fact—just the whole ball of dirty wax.[28]

Groder was warden of the Federal Center for Correctional Research in Butner, North Carolina. In the session described above, it was Groder against eight inmates. In other groups, it would be a dozen of Groder's trained group members against a single inmate. Several court cases of inmates compelled to take part in these programs are still pending. The START program in Missouri described earlier which was closed by the Federal Bureau of Prisons following the threat of lawsuits, involved a similar kind of "attack therapy." The conditioning in these sessions is no stronger than is used routinely in Synanon or one or the many other voluntary facilities for drug users. If anything, the abuse is more devastating and focused in the Synanon groups because the people in it are more skillful and experienced in applying these procedures. As with the electric shock mentioned earlier, the only difference between the Synanon approach and the illegal START methods is that one is voluntary and the other isn't. If these programs are actually as successful as their proponents claim, they should be made more available to child molesters in the community. The way society operates today, there are very few adult child molesters who can be very happy with their present mode of sexual adjustment. The price they pay in mental suffering is tragically high. Being able to enter voluntary programs, even using shock, without stigma and a police presence, would probably do more to reduce child molesting than similar measures after incarceration. Of course, dealing with this question adequately requires a critical examination of morals laws and the discriminatory way in which they are applied, and of the morbid fascination of the media, especially television, with brutality and sexual domination.

Like other promising innovations, the legitimacy of behavior modification was undermined by its association with imprisonment. No psychologist can practice behavior modification in a prison and still follow accepted ethical guidelines of informed voluntary consent. At best a psychologist can fall back upon the rationalization used at the Somers, Connecticut, institution—that behavior modification was the only treatment for child molesters available. It is hard to criticize the only show in town. However, the significance of the statement can only be understood in the light of the absurd policies of incarcerating sex offenders in large, isolated institutions which seem to encourage the very crimes for which these people are imprisoned. Child molesting itself is probably not encouraged by imprisonment, unless one extends this to the common practice of experienced cons forcing an attractive young inmate to submit to sexual advances, but it is in no way relieved by a long spell behind bars without much to do except daydream.

Right Over Wrong

It is much easier to direct behavior by telling a person when he is right than by telling him when he is wrong. Pointing out positive instances is more helpful because they constitute a smaller class of events. It is easier to learn what a triangle is by having one pointed out than it is by being told what a triangle is not. A simple demonstration that is easily repeated illustrates this principle. Select two objects in a room, use one of them as the test object for Method 1 and the other for Method 2. Bring a person into the room and tell him he is supposed to locate an object you have selected. Whenever he is on the wrong track, you will say "wrong." As the person walks around the room and looks in various directions and touches things, you say "wrong" every time he heads in the wrong direction, picks up the wrong object, opens the wrong cupboard, etc. This is a very frustrating task for the finder and a brutal task for the director. In the second procedure, the person is brought into the room and asked to search for another object. This time the director will tell him "right" whenever he is on the right track and say nothing when he is wrong. When the person starts walking in the right direction or looking in the right area or opening the right cupboard, the director says "right." This is a much happier task for both. It is also a much more effective method in that the person will find the hidden object more quickly. There are a number of reasons why it is more efficient to tell a person when he is on the right track. For one thing, there is the constant interpersonal friction of saying "wrong, wrong, wrong," which makes it seem that the person cannot do anything right. With a multiplicity of choices, it is easier to reward the single right path than punish the innumerable wrong ones.

The superiority of positive reinforcement over punishment has significant implications for handling offenders in any kind of institutional setting. The way things presently work, the jail inmate is left alone by the guards if he does his own time and follows the rules. He is given no special praise or recognition. Perhaps in a year's time if he has a clean record, a prison board, *if they are aware he has been following the rules,* may grant him increased privileges. However, the connection between his good behavior and the reward is so tenuous, vague, and remote that it loses almost all its power as a reinforcer. In the main the jail operates on the principle of punishment. The inmate is constantly being told "wrong, wrong, wrong" and rarely told that he is doing anything right. Even when the correctness of some of his actions is eventually admitted, this is balanced and outweighed by acts of omission ("Although you have been working steady in the shops you haven't been enrolled in any educational programs").

According to Philip Zimbardo, the lack of clear criteria for good behavior destroys the inmate's sense of the future. Convicts do not know what they have to do to get out. They can get negative reports but never a positive report.

> They behave in a certain way which gets them a (disciplinary) report, and it is only the absence of negative reports that is judged. That is, they are judged to be clean as long as they haven't done anything bad. But there is nothing in any of the reports I have seen or any of the statements where there is something specific they can do positively on any given day. Not only no programs, but there are no explicit criteria that the disciplinary committee gives them or that the parole board gives them: "If you do A, B, C, D by this time period, this will be the result." That could give people a purpose, give them a future orientation.[29]

Zimbardo believes that criminality is directly related to a weakened sense of the future. No deterrent can be effective unless a person can project himself into the time frame when punishment will occur. All imprisonment that is arbitrary and capricious tends to weaken the inmate's sense of control over his own destiny. Living from day to day in prison is poor training for life outside.

When I first became involved in correctional issues I thought there was a real place for behavior mod in the prison system. It seemed to be a way of making explicit contracts between the inmate and the staff, of getting rewards and punishments out in the open. After seeing what happened in the START program in Missouri and Groder's "attack therapy," I have reluctantly come to the conclusion that there is no place for these programs in prison. The problem is not with the methods themselves or with the people using them, but with the coercive environment in which they are used. There can be no such thing as an ethical means of behavior change in a concentration camp. Though there are differences between the Nazi extermination camps and the American prisons of today, inmates in both institutions lack rights, staff have absolute power, the courts adopt a hands-off attitude, and what happens inside is hidden from public view.

Behavior modification can play a significant role outside prison in dealing with many of the problems that get people into trouble with the law. Just as heroin addicts submit themselves to the incredible verbal abuse of the Synanon session, a thirty-year-old man with an urge to molest children or assault young women might be induced to undertake a systematic behavior modification program if his name did not go on police records. Teodoro Ayllon, who developed the first token economy, has left institutional work in favor of community practice. He sees the goal of behavior therapy as providing techniques for individuals to control themselves. In place of nonverbal "shaping" procedures, in which the discovery of the correct behavior is a matter of trial and error, Ayllon advocates instructions plus reinforcement. Without instructions, conditioning is tedious and often ineffective, since it treats a person like a bird or a rat. For Ayllon's clients the reinforcement system is explicit and rational. The individual knows what he is supposed to do in order to obtain a reward. Nothing is taken away from him that he had before. He learns to apportion to himself something that he likes (drinking a cocktail before dinner or watching TV) with something he has difficulty motivating himself to do (cleaning the house or going through the work day without a drink). The behavior therapist and the patient agree on the reinforcement schedule to be used.

UNREALIZED POTENTIAL OF RESEARCH

9

Few prisons to this day maintain resident research staffs, and fewer still have the resources to justify more than that research which is directly relevant to prison administrative and bookkeeping procedures. The academic research community, on the other hand, has either found the prison inaccessible as a research laboratory or, more generally, to be a marginal setting involving low academic prestige and high anxiety.

PETER C. BUFFUM

In most sectors of society, research has been a significant force for change. In corrections, research has been a means of preserving the status quo; its primary use has been to justify the appropriations of government agencies. The major output of "research departments" is voluminous tabulations of arrests, convictions, incarcerations, and recidivism classified by age, sex, race, county, type of offense, and every other conceivable characteristic. Such reports are full of minor details and impoverished with respect to explanations and solutions. The major reason for this sterility is the schism between research and action. The people charged with undertaking studies have no responsibility for solving problems. Research unrelated to action tends to become hermetic and irrelevant. Too many correctional researchers have become clerks and flacks whose primary allegiance is to their employers rather than to a code of professional ethics. In other fields this has created a niche for counter-researchers—professionals outside the establishment developing plans for social change and trying them out on a modest scale. But because of limited access to institutions, inmates, or staff, it is extremely difficult to be a counter-researcher in corrections. The only remaining role is that of critic. Critics are necessary, but they cannot substitute for researchers *within the system* working for change. While General Motors has thousands of workers and millions of dollars invested in models presently rolling off the assembly line, and paid lobbyists to combat any attempt to tighten emission or safety standards, it also has a large research department working on new prototypes. These researchers are men and women specifically hired to work for change. That the new technological innovations do not get implemented as rapidly as some would hope is a commentary on the oligopolistic nature of the automobile industry; promising innovations can be kept off the market for a limited period even though the company has paid for their development.

So much of what passes for correctional research consists of tabulations of the most superficial sort. It is doubtful that a single jail is going to be changed because 75 per cent of its inmates are repeaters. There isn't going to be any investigation or any firings. But let an inmate from a prominent family hang himself or be gang raped, and someone will have to answer for it. Reform of penal institutions has developed more from scandal than from research. The main reason research has had so little impact is that researchers have asked trivial questions and are kept out of policy issues. No one can disagree with the need for accurate statistics and record-keeping; precise counts will enable an agency to see what kind of job it is doing. However, a researcher has a responsibility that goes beyond bare statistical tabulation in a field with accessible programs, where change is possible and necessary. Corrections differs from astronomy, where research activities are largely restricted to tabulating the pre-ordained paths of heavenly bodies. Most of us assume that the movement of men and women through the correctional system is influenced by more proximate forces. The collection, tabulation, and analysis of statistics cannot be excluded, but these activities are not sufficient for the research enterprise. In this field particularly, a researcher is obliged to get involved in programs for change. Regarding expensive reports and plans-to-plan, the experience of Seattle with mass transit is instructive. When the city council considered the idea of implementing a free bus service to central Seattle, it found that a feasibility study would cost $60,000. Rather than put this money into another report, the council invested it in a subsidy for a free bus system which demonstrated in practice not only the system's feasibility, but its success.

Correctional research tends to have a managerial bias, in that the criteria used to measure program success favor institutional adjustment. Occasionally this bias is subtle and indirect, as in the survey of the conjugal visiting program at Parchman (Mississippi) Prison.[1] This was a well-intentioned survey of the attitudes of inmates and guards towards the program. The author asked people whether conjugal visits made inmates cooperate more and work harder, or whether it weakened trust among inmates. But the critical question was touched upon only indirectly. The Parchman program has been in operation over thirty years and is not only the oldest in the nation but one of the few extant. In 1975 only two states have conjugal visiting, and only the Parchman program reaches a sizable number of inmates. The riddle then becomes not the dynamics of Parchman but why the other 99 per cent of prisons have not adopted this humane measure. The answer lies in the paleological belief that sexual deprivation is part of the punishment. This is rarely expressed covertly by correctional officials, who justify their opposition to conjugal visiting on grounds of security and potential conflict arising from prisoners who do not have wives. However these problems have been overcome in Parchman, where the program is strongly endorsed by single as well as married inmates.

Mexican prisons have long established conjugal visiting programs that include not only wives but also women friends and prostitutes.[2]

The problems of undertaking research in a penal system that has undergone dozens of investigations by Congress, state legislators, the American Bar Association, and various federal and private task forces should not be underestimated. Officials have learned either to give the right answers or to give none at all. In 1970 a survey of prison disturbances was undertaken under the aegis of the American Correctional Association, an organization of prison officials. A letter was sent out by a committee chairman of the ACA who also happened to be director of the South Carolina Department of Corrections. Even with this official backing, fewer than one-third of the institutions surveyed responded, even to the extent of stating that they had nothing to report.[3] Silence, delay, and red tape are among the favorite tactics of correctional officials in dealing with inquiries. The problems of attempting to obtain information within the constraints of a one-year study are obvious. Hit-and-run surveys by outside agencies are likely to be limited or biased in terms of the people interviewed, the questions asked, and the respondents' belief (or lack of belief) in the confidentiality of their answers. It isn't easy to question an inmate (or a guard) with several uniformed guards hovering nearby. The basis of prison architecture is that a person is never beyond the sight of the custodial staff. It is extraordinarily difficult to conduct an interview in a special lawyer's room when one is separated from the inmate by a glass wall and converses by telephone. One cannot put aside the thought that the conversation is being overheard or recorded by a third party. The only feasible research strategy is to spend enough time within the prison to enable people to gain trust and the researcher to learn who can be trusted and when and where to ask questions. Otherwise the interviewer is going to be "conned" by staff as well as inmates. The reserve and even disdain of correctional staff and inmates alike towards survey research is somewhat understandable in view of its dismal record in producing tangible reforms. A prison official could spend his entire day filling out surveys and questionnaires without accomplishing anything worthwhile. A research strategy is required that ties information-seeking to policy change. Any survey that does not link these two stages inextricably is going to fail, especially in a field which has been so often surveyed. Sociologist Edith Flynn believes that surveys, by raising hopes and expectations without delivering tangible improvements, contribute to prison unrest.

> Finding themselves at the receiving end of countless visits, surveys, and investigative inquiries, administrators and wardens can attest to the fact that prisons are being extensively studied while sufficient funding for the implementation of the recommended reforms never materializes. Inmates observe legislators, investigative teams, and the press come and go, only to see real or perceived gains fade into psychological losses when they are compared with the harsh realities of their existence.[4]

Daniel Glaser,[5] who has spent several decades moving between the two worlds of the correctional administrator and the academic researcher, recommends the use of small-scale experiments coupled with evaluation programs as a means of improving correctional practice. Accepting the fragmentation of the various parts of the system, he believes that piecemeal innovation is the most viable strategy. An important consideration is that these small studies must be undertaken with a commitment to improve the entire system. Otherwise the researcher's efforts become compartmentalized and isolated from the main system and will disappear once the project is terminated or the innovator departs. Research must be embedded in program operation without being used merely to justify it.

In mental hospitals I was usually able to assume good will on the part of administrators towards my research. If I had an idea for a program that would help patients or staff, they would probably let me try it out on a small scale after we went through the customary red tape. This kind of mutual trust is absent from my dealings with wardens. It is not that they are evil or stupid, but rather that their association with a failed institution has made them incredibly defensive about criticism.

No matter what is proposed, there will be someone who doesn't like it. The easiest thing is to do nothing. This defensiveness, occasionally bordering on paranoia, will thwart any impulse to experiment unless someone else is going to bear total responsibility. This was one of the strongest arguments for inviting the federal government (LEAA) into an area that has been traditionally under state and local jurisdiction. Unfortunately, the potential of money and servicçs from LEAA has not been realized. It may be useful to review some of the reasons for this.

Unlike the mental health field, where grants went to academic investigators, most of whom were affiliated with universities or private foundations, the federal money in corrections was suborned by state agencies and committees controlled by law enforcement personnel. The infusion of new money did not have the same stimulus value that it had in mental health, where it brought in new people. Proposals were often considered by committees for their political implications. At the outset LEAA failed to employ the peer-review procedures developed by HEW. Instead it relied heavily on state councils, where politicians and police exercise considerable influence. There was a tremendous competition for funds between line and staff personnel and between hardware and software. Most organizations contain line employees who produce goods and deliver actual service and staff employees who provide backup services. In the typical prison, the warden and guards are line employees, while vocational counselors, physicians, and psychologists are staff. In a power struggle between line and staff, the line employees tend to win. Proposals to put money into hardware systems, such as electronic monitors, computerized information systems, and heavy armaments, have been favored over investments in people programs. Most money has gone to more of the same, but the newer and more sophisticated model.

Many of the critical questions about imprisonment have not even been asked, much less answered. There has been virtually no serious documentation of the effects of imprisonment upon guards and other staff members. We often act as if only prisoners are affected by the harsh conditions of confinement and ignore its effects on the thousands of employees who spend their working days behind bars. For information about the effects of incarceration we must rely on impression and anecdote. When I became involved in a court suit attacking solitary confinement, I examined the psychological, psychiatric, and medical literature to see what was known. I found very little that was directly relevant. In the two centuries since solitary confinement was used for offenders in the Walnut Street Prison, there has been virtually no systematic evaluation of its effects. Considering all the money that has gone towards research, all the trivial topics that have been studied to death, this omission borders on scandal. The information available about solitary confinement consists of anecdotes from former prisoners and explorers, or experimental studies of college students and astronauts isolated for long periods in other kinds of situations. Inmates who have described their experiences tend to be exceptional individuals who survived the harsh treatment in reasonably good shape. Studies of astronauts and aquanauts are interesting, but these are highly selected volunteers with excellent morale rather than people incarcerated to be punished. Nor is the example set by monks, hermits, saints, or other self-chosen isolates particularly relevant to arrested offenders. Their example can justify anything, including flagellation and mutilation. The material on sensory deprivation is well documented, but the environment in The Hole is noisy, smelly, and brutal rather than stimulus-deprived. Research with animals has shown that isolation during the early formative years has serious consequences afterwards. This is not particularly relevant to the predicament of the adult offender.

I have found that this lack of applicable research extends to every area of imprisonment. The situation is somewhat better in parole and probation, but in prisons the researchers rarely have gone beyond classification. The occasional study of "treatment outcome" generally finds no results. Detailed investigations of the inmate society, such as those by Clemmer,[6] Sykes,[7] and Goffman,[8] are important in showing how inmates are socialized into the prison, but they do not try to solve any of the problems they unearth.

It is necessary to explain why research, which has played such an important role in improving other sorts of institutions, has been trivial and sometimes sinister in prison. This is neither accidental nor merely a cultural lag. Research is truth-seeking; and this sort of activity cannot flourish in a repressive atmosphere. Whatever its obvious limitations in other areas, American society has been the leader in both technological and social innovation. For the last two hundred years we have been an experimenting society. This refers less to official policy, which tends to be conservative, then to the actions of individuals, groups, and organizations. The laissez-faire attitude of government on most issues has permitted a tremendous amount of experimentation. The school system of the nation may be in some difficulty, but there are literally thousands of educational experiments going on at any time, not only formal research projects, but "experiments in nature" or contrasting systems existing side by side, following Summerhill, Montessori, B. F. Skinner, and the English Infant School. The same multiplicity of practices and policies characterizes the fragmented correctional services. There are many aspects of the federal correctional system that are extremely progressive. At a campus of my own university the government is currently paying tuition, board, and living expenses for twenty federal inmates. They are free to move about the campus on their own but must return to supervised quarters in the evening. Several states have decriminalized the possession of marijuana and thereby reduced the likelihood of stigmatizing an entire generation. Numerous states are experimenting with public service alternatives to imprisonment. Minnesota officials have recognized the Prisoners Union as a legitimate representative of inmates and have begun negotiating with it. Innumerable other innovations are currently in progress. Public works alternatives have been used successfully for so long that they are no longer in the category of experiments. What characterizes most of this work is that *virtually all of the programs with successful results have taken place outside penal institutions*.

Prison is a poor place to do research into human behavior for the same reason that the zoo is a poor place to do research on animal behavior. The conditions of confinement warp the behavior to such an extent that it is virtually unrecognizable. One is studying institutional adaptations in a bizarre environment. The applicability of most of this research, except perhaps to other oppressive settings, is minimal. Rampant homosexuality in all American prisons provides no information on the sexual proclivities of offenders in the outside world. The same lesson was learned years ago when Solly Zuckerman documented a wide range of baboon behaviors in the London Zoo that were infrequent or nonexistent in the animal's natural habitat.[9] Considering all the money and resources that have gone into developing and maintaining zoos, remarkably little good information about animal behavior has come forth. Most of this research has been devoted to ways of keeping captive animals alive and looking decent. The purpose of the work is to maintain the viability of the zoo as an institution. This function is very similar to that of the correctional researcher, whose efforts have gone to justify existing budgets and keeping institutions running smoothly.

In theory a prison population would be a researcher's dream. There is a large number of people in a relatively fixed and homogeneous environment for long periods, on whom there is ample background information available; people who have a great deal of spare time, and who work long hours for little money. What more could a psychologist want in the way of a research population? Plenty more, when it comes right down to it. The essential ingredient of research, the spirit of free inquiry, is totally absent in the prison. In actual fact, research on prisoners has contributed virtually nothing to psychological research or theory. The punitive, oppressive atmosphere of the prison handicaps the researcher in the design and conduct of the study, it reduces the inmates' willingness to cooperate voluntarily, and it limits the range of topics that can be studied. In the previous discussion of behavior modification, I briefly alluded to the unethical nature of any kind of psychotherapy that might be carried out in a concentration camp. The same strictures apply to research. In the Hitler era, concentration camp inmates became guinea pigs in human experimentation. Extremely barbaric experiments were performed on unwilling victims or ''volunteers'' who hoped to secure a little extra food or some special privileges. The most compelling lesson concerns the abuses of fundamental medical ethics that can occur in the name of research, but it is noteworthy too that no discoveries of any significance came out of these experiments. I do not feel that this was mere accident or incompetence, due to the stupidity of the physicians who undertook these immoral experiments. The unethical nature of the entire operation was inimical to the search for truth. It poisoned the tree of knowledge at its roots, and all the investigators found were dead limbs, peeling bark, and fallen leaves. The writings of most significance that came out of these inhuman places were the personal notes of former inmates such as Bruno Bettelheim [10] and Viktor Frankl [11] which have enriched our understanding of the survival of the human spirit. It also may turn out that the prison writings of most enduring value are not those by wardens, penologists, researchers, or reformers, but those of inmates. It is ludicrous to speak of positive character change and relevant job training in the cesspool atmosphere of Rikers Island and Joliet. Research will have to focus on methods of keeping offenders out of such places while still providing some protection to the larger society. This will not be an easy task, but it is not impossible. The effort cannot be hobbled by unrealistic requirements of success. Reforming offenders in a chaotic society is a difficult task at best. The minimum criterion of success would be a lower recidivism rate than is found in other programs. There will be many failures but hopefully far fewer than in the present system. America today has the highest homicide rate in the western world. New programs should not be required to eliminate homicides completely, but only to reduce them below present levels. This would be the initial requirement. Beyond that, as the programs become well established, more rigorous requirements can be set. However, researchers should not be expected to do the impossible overnight. Among Seabees, a military unit with high morale, there was a saying that the improbable could be done in a short time, the impossible would take a while longer.

Research can play an important part in evaluating the effectiveness of community alternatives. We can learn how halfway houses are working in Portland and Cincinnati before identical programs are funded in a hundred other cities. All too often we make use of these evaluations after the promising innovation has died or has become so ossified as to resist change. The sensationalism of the media and the faddishness of government agencies interfere with the rational assessment of programs. The rush to receive credit for innovation often leads to the premature acceptance of a bad idea or the warping of a good idea. Some of the most brutal and ineffective aspects of our present penal system were hailed as promising innovations and replicated innumerable times before anyone knew how they actually worked. Researchers will play an important role in reforming the penal system when they start asking important questions and involve themselves directly in programs of institutional change.

Prison researchers cannot be expected to make a dent in the larger political and social inequalities. Poverty, racism, parental neglect, poor schools, and inadequate housing combine to bring individuals into conflict with the law. For the time being, the best the correctional researcher can do is to indicate the causative role of these factors. The special province and expertise of the correctional researcher is in the handling of offenders. At the least he or she is responsible for seeing that the offender is made no worse because of contacts with the criminal justice system. This is similar to Florence Nightingale's dictum that the first purpose of the hospital is to do the sick no harm. Correctional researchers are still a long way from achieving even this minimal objective.

It would be distracting at this point to engage in a lengthy discussion of reform versus revolution. The orientation of this book is much more evolutionary than revolutionary. In a dynamic system, all institutions and all problems are connected. A change in one part of the system will have ramifications in all other parts. I cannot fault an organization attempting to provide jobs for ex-cons because it is not at the same time doing anything about tax reform or air pollution. There are many problems that need to be worked on, and they are all connected at some level. This interrelationship of all institutions and problems has immobilized some people, who perceive their alternatives as changing everything or changing nothing. The ecological lesson of interdependency has a hopeful side. If everything is connected, a change in one part of the system will have reverberations elsewhere. When a group starts looking for jobs for ex-cons, they come up directly against unemployment, housing discrimination, and irrational parole rules. Following the search for jobs long enough, the group will eventually have to deal with air pollution and tax reform too. The important thing is to begin working for immediate tangible reforms in the context of long-range solutions.

There can be no clear line between basic and applied research. We already know that crime and imprisonment are correlated most highly with age (young), education (poor), social class (low), race (nonwhite), family background (broken home), gender (male), geography (urban), and marital status (single). In view of these relationships, research aimed at identifying future criminals (high-risk individuals) is likely, given the high rate of error of previous studies, to stigmatize vast numbers of young people at an early age. Even if some researcher should demonstrate that a chromosomal abnormality is related to some people's violent outbursts, this would explain only a tiny fraction of criminal behavior. It would have no relevance to the extensive amount of white-collar crime, drug abuse, morals offenses, drunk and vagrancy charges, car theft, or most burglaries and robberies. This is a field where biological reductionism in the form of theories about bad brains and weak genes has a long and ignoble history. At the present time, the biggest payoff will come from research directly tied to policy change. Researchers can also play a valuable role in cutting through the semantic jungle, clarifying the model muddle, and getting paleologic out into the open. Psychiatrists and psychologists are uniquely equipped as professionals to deal rationally with paleologic.

THE MENTAL HOSPITAL CONNECTION

10

"The state hospitals were doing a magnificent job in pioneering efforts towards miraculous recoveries for many patients," Sheriff Canlis declared. "There were 37,000 adults in state mental hospitals before Lanterman-Petris-Short. Now there are less than 7,000. Where are these people now? . . . Many are in county jails. Many are in state prisons."

In the 1950s, the president of the American Psychiatric Association issued a facetious call for blowing up mental hospitals. Another prominent psychiatrist, Karl Menninger, proposed that state officials invest their money in brains instead of bricks. Twenty years later, a federal task force on criminal justice came forth with its slogan to plan, not build; and the director of the California Department of Corrections told a legislative committee that the only solution to San Quentin was 200 pounds of TNT. Although many parallels exist between the situation in mental hospitals two decades ago and the situation in corrections today, it is surprising how little attention has been paid by those in prison work to the recent precedent of mental hospital reform. As Goffman [1] and Etzioni [2] have demonstrated, the dynamics of total institutions can be studied in evolutionary and comparative terms. In this chapter, I will discuss these parallels with a clear warning that I am talking about the dialectics of institutions rather than the relevance of psychiatry to corrections. Inmates do *not* believe that they are in prison to be treated for mental disorders, and staff do not feel qualified to administer such treatments. A misapplication of a medical model to corrections has produced euphemism, tokenism, and, occasionally, barbarism. There is no safe and effective medical treatment for criminality.

Disenchantment with warehousing mental patients came shortly after the Second World War. Some of the credit is due to those conscientious objectors who worked on hospital wards in lieu of military service. Appalled at the treatment society provided for its mentally ill, these articulate young men gained access to the media.* Their efforts were supported by such journalists as Albert Deutsch, who documented the deplorable conditions and brutality.[3] America's mental institutions, once advocated so eloquently by Dorothea Lynd Dix [4] and other humanitarians, had over the decades become a combination of hospitals for treating the mentally ill, colonies for the impaired, old folks' homes, and dumping grounds for a great variety of social problems.[5] The problem was compounded by a serious model muddle which produced unclear and often contradictory purposes. Press reports of brutality, exploitation of patients, overcrowding, and inadequate facilities aroused many citizens, who petitioned their state legislators to act. Reform was made easier by several developments occuring in the late 1940s. The discovery of tranquilizing drugs permitted the elimination of physical restraints such as the straightjacket, chloroform, and the "sick needle." Almost overnight, tranquilizers

* There is an interesting parallel to the situation in the 1960s, when large numbers of educated middle-class white youth were arrested on drug charges and saw the inside of jails. To what extent this contributed to the prison reform movement is difficult to say. For the most part, it resulted in a reform of drug laws intended primarily to keep these educated middle-class white youths out of jail.

transformed the madhouse and made possible the introduction of psychotherapy and activity programs for patients who had previously been regarded as hopeless.

The possibility of discharging chronic patients into the community produced an emphasis on treatment rather than custody. It was no longer sufficient for a superintendent to demand new buildings when wards became overcrowded. Hospital administrators found themselves judged on the basis of discharge rates rather than the size of the dairy herd and the state of the gardens. There was an upgrading of the responsibilities, training, and salaries of nurses and attendants. Morale at all levels of the staff improved dramatically as patients were discharged. An emphasis on treatment created the need for social workers to help place patients in the community and for psychiatrists, psychologists, and occupational therapists. This influx of new professionals created a more democratic staff structure. Caste lines became blurred as treatment skills were applied on the wards and in halfway houses rather than exclusively in medical offices. Progressive institutions made widespread use of volunteers. Special programs were developed to recruit college students for part time work and summer jobs. Finally, there was an influx of new money and of people who became the research and development arms of the reform movement.

Initially there was great uncertainty as to priorities. The Second World War had produced a hiatus in construction, and there was strong pressure upon legislators to replace obsolete, overcrowded buildings. Programs for upgrading nursing skills and training paraprofessionals were urgently needed. The federal government, through the National Institute of Mental Health, responded generously with grants for long-range planning, training, and for upgrading facilities. To encourage innovation, the Hospital Improvement Program (HIP) was launched. Each institution was entitled to a million dollars for innovative programs to be spread over a decade. Much of the money went to institutions totally unprepared for change. A custodial staff was suddenly faced with an influx of new personnel and programs dedicated to discharging patients. Turmoil arose as the old routines were disrupted.

Previously, virtually all the treatment had taken place on the admission wards, where the professional staff was concentrated. The chronic wards were an accumulation of those patients who had not responded to treatments for decades. I worked on chronic wards where the average length of stay exceeded twenty-five years per patient. Now suddenly a great optimism about changing things reached the back wards. Sizable numbers of long-stay patients were discharged directly from chronic wards to halfway houses, boarding homes, and back to their own families.

The courts and the legislatures assisted the reform movement. A series of court decisions expanded patient rights, and legislation was passed making commitment more difficult. Budget-conscious legislators were impressed by the potential savings resulting from placing patients in community programs rather than keeping them in institutions. The actual savings turned out to be largely illusory but the figures looked good on paper. All across the nation there was a concerted effort to reduce the size of the warehouses and in some cases to close them down. In a five-year period beginning in 1967, New York State reduced its mental hospital population from 80,000 to 44,000. Alabama cut its hospital population in half following a court order stating that a mental patient had a constitutional right to treatment. California started somewhat earlier than other states in de-institutionalizing care of mental patients. Between 1955 and 1975, it reduced its patient population from 50,000 to 7,000 and was hoping to get out of warehousing entirely.

With the flood of discharged patients, the lack of treatment facilities in the community became apparent. There was considerable resistance from communities affected by the hospital closings, who saw themselves losing in two ways. First, they were losing the employees payroll, and second, they were becoming the dumping grounds for the discharged patients. Citizens of the small community of Long Beach, New York, woke up to find 700 discharged mental patients living in their midst. In Manhattan, mental patients drifted to the welfare hotels off Times Square and into depressed sections of the Upper West Side.

Proprietary nursing homes lacking in necessary psychiatric and nursing services sprang up adjacent to the closed hospitals. Disputes arose between state and city agencies as to the responsibility for discharged patients and the regulation of the nursing homes. Numerous investigations revealed that little was being done to provide therapy or recreation for patients living in the community. A team of investigators in Canada found that discharged mental patients in boarding homes spent most of their time in the bedrooms.[6] Many were not allowed kitchen privileges or use of living rooms. They were as isolated socially as they had been in institutions. Hospital employees, including psychiatrists and psychologists, who thought they had secure jobs, suddenly found themselves unemployed as institutions began cutting back services. Hospital staff lobbied at state capitols against plans for closing down additional institutions. They argued that helpless and sometimes dangerous mental patients were being turned loose on the community. By 1975 the situation had reached a stalemate in which the closure of older institutions had ceased, but no new ones were being constructed.

Lessons for the Prison

Resistance of the institution lobby to closing down prisons has already surfaced. When the governor of California attempted to close down the unnecessary medium-security facility at Susanville, local citizens protested to their state senator, who applied enough pressure to keep it open. Whether by accident or design, the California Department of Corrections embarked upon a determined program to limit parole and keep people in institutions longer. In 1971 almost three-quarters of the inmates going up for parole hearings were granted release dates, but this fell to under 20 per cent in 1972. It would be a serious mistake to underestimate the political and economic strength of the institutional lobby. Corrections is a multi-billion-dollar business, and most of this money is tied up in institutions. Prison employees receive low wages for doing dirty jobs, but if they are told that their jobs are unnecessary, they become angry and upset and apply what political leverage they have towards protecting their livelihood. Most prison employees believe that their skills have little utility in the outside world, but in fact, the deplorable state of jails, drunk tanks, and other places of short-term detention will require more and better-trained personnel. This is a niche that trained prison employees can fill. It is wasteful and harmful to staff city and county jails with police and deputy sheriffs who dislike this work.

Programs to de-institutionalize staff roles would be extremely helpful in overcoming the opposition of prison employees to the closure of large warehouses. Employees should be required to participate in parole and probation work and to spend time in short-term detention facilities before the large institutions are closed out from under them without their having acquired usable job skills. It will not be easy to transform guards into parole officers, but it is a practicable objective. It is the worst kind of idealistic thinking (psychological reductionism) to believe that guards are "the wrong sort of people." Put into the right sort of job and given the proper encouragement, training, and supervision, most will be able to handle that job. The same kind of situation ensued when mental hospitals changed from custody to treatment. Most of the old-line nurses and attendants were able to make the transition successfully. Those who weren't were either transferred, kicked upstairs, or left voluntarily. A few had to be dismissed after acrimonious disputes over their handling new responsibilities in old ways.

Another lesson from the mental hospital experience concerns the timing and location of the closures. It did not necessarily happen that the oldest and largest institutions were the first to close. Occasionally the reverse occurred. Some of the larger and more unwieldy institutions were subdivided into regional units, and the smaller institutions were closed. This may sound paradoxical in view of the universal condemnation of large facilities, but it made sense in terms of political realities. There were more jobs and contracts at stake in a large institution than in a small one. When political and budgetary considerations were pitted against logic, votes and money tended to win. Mendocino State Hospital, the most dynamic and effective and the smallest of the California mental hospitals, became one of the first to close. It was the dedication of the staff in reducing the patient population to a third of its previous size that doomed the hospital. It was easier for the state administrators to redistribute its remaining patients than to close one of the larger, less efficient institutions. In Saskatchewan, where I also worked, it was the smaller and more progressive of the two state hospitals that was closed.

The courts played a seminal role in the campaign to close down the mental hospitals through their decisions requiring mimimum standards of treatment. Although court decisions have labeled certain types of imprisonment to be cruel and unusual punishment, and in the case of Arkansas declared the entire penal system to be unconstitutional, no attempt has been made to enforce such sweeping decisions. More likely, the courts will make it more expensive for the state to confine inmates and thereby make community supervision more attractive to budget-conscious legislators. Inmate rights are being constantly expanded through court decisions. This has been a slow process involving mainly the less controversial rights such as religion, the press (the right to receive certain periodicals), and mail from lawyers. Perhaps the greatest immediate contribution that the courts can make to prison reform would be to hold the state responsible for the consequences of incarceration. If the state sees fit to deprive people of their liberty for several years, it should be responsible for the effects of their incarceration. Significant damage awards to inmates who have been living in overcrowded, badly ventilated, and vermin-ridden facilities will impel state officials to take prompt remedial action. However, the courts are not likely to make decisions which will bring them into direct confrontation with the executive or legislative branches. Court decisions which appear to be broad and sweeping are valuable more for their educational value in preparing the way for long-range changes than in their immediate impact.

Inmates in Swedish prisons keep virtually all of their civil rights intact, including the right to vote. It is difficult to predict what the effects might be of allowing American inmates to vote, particularly in the rural areas where many large institutions are located. Leavenworth County in Kansas has state, federal, civil, and military prisons whose residents could conceivably elect inmate legislators, or at least people favorable to inmate rights. While this might encourage political rivalry within institutions, it would be a more constructive arena for group activity than stabbings, extortion, and riots. When the Supreme Court ruled in 1971 that inmates should have access to law libraries, prison officials feared that this might raise the level of tension. They predicted that "jailhouse lawyers" would encourage inmates to send in unrealistic writs, and disturbances would erupt when these were rejected. Fortunately, these fears, like those of prison officials against inmate religious associations such as the Muslims, have proven unfounded. Access to a law library has provided a focal point for inmate energies. As one prison official described it, "Instead of becoming a serious problem, as we thought it might, jailhouse law has actually served as a calming influence. If an inmate can vent his hostility in legal briefs filed in the courts, he is less likely to be a disruptive influence in the prison population." [7] The brunt of the increase in inmate appeals has been borne by the courts rather than the prison system. This activity emphasizes the low level of legitimacy that the prison has for those incarcerated. If inmates felt that their convictions, sentences, and conditions of confinement were fair and deserved, all this appeal writing would not be taking place.

The salutary influence of a professional staff is another lesson of the mental hospital experience. More psychologists, social workers, and counselors with allegiances that extend beyond the institution can serve as a counterweight to arbitrary administrative action. It is not likely that a state corrections commissioner would flinch today if his agency were blacklisted by the American Psychological Association or the American Association of Social Workers. In the future, with more professional people involved, the threat of the blacklist would give professional employees greater leverage to develop adequate programs. More use of volunteers from the community as well as from universities would be desirable. Every person who becomes aware of what is happening in the prison system in a potential force for change, though care must be taken to insure that the lessons of visits to penal institutions are not directed into justifications for more buildings and more staff. Thousands of students in universities across the country would welcome the opportunity for part-time or summer work in correctional institutions. The defensiveness of most corrections departments keeps them from drawing upon this large pool of motivated and intelligent young people. Fortunately there are some exceptions. In 1974, faculty from fifteen Oregon colleges taught courses inside correctional institutions. Oregon State Penitentiary offers more college courses per year to its 1249 inmates than any other prison in the nation. The program is organized by the Oregon Department of Corrections; travel expenses for the instructors and books for the inmates are provided by local institutions. Between 1971 and 1974, students from a majority of the state's colleges and universities worked in over forty criminal justice agencies or programs. The state civil service commission gives preference in regular hiring to students who have worked in the program. It is too early to say how many of these students will choose the criminal justice field for careers. Students bring enthusiasm and fresh ideas into a setting where most people have become stultified in their attitudes and practices. Nothing much is likely to happen if only one college student comes into this kind of setting, but if six work together, they can support one another.

Detention Without Cure

There still remains a reluctance to call mental institutions "hospitals," because they don't cure patients. In a very literal sense, this is true. The patient who comes in voluntarily or is committed for several weeks or months *is not going to be cured during her stay*. For the most part, we do not know what causes mental disorders and have no specific cures. Instead she is detained until her immediate state of confusion or depression lifts to the extent that she can behave acceptably in society. The treatment goal is the relief of an immediate stress response. There is no possibility of a long-term overhaul of character in two weeks or two months. The middle-aged man undergoing a severe depression who cannot be treated outside will be given psychoactive drugs to lift his mood, but there is no pretense on anyone's part that this is a long-term cure. As in the case of a heart attack, the goal of intervention is to relieve the immediate symtoms and return the patient home with the realization that he is probably going to experience further attacks. We try to insure that the patient is *not* changed in any fundamental way by his hospital stay. This significant step has required the elimination of hospital-induced pathologies including serious infection, abuse, and social disruption. Except in the case of very young children, a short stay in hospital probably isn't going to do too much harm. A long stay in hospital is an entirely different matter.

It is instructive to see what has happened to psychiatry since the abandonment of warehousing as a social policy. Cures for schizophrenia, depression, alcoholism, and the disorders of old age—the major illnesses that brought people into mental hospitals—have not been found. Such disorders are at least as prevalent as they used to be. The major change is that we handle patients differently. We deprive fewer people of their civil rights and disrupt their lives to a lesser degree. There are still mental hospitals treating patients, most of whom are voluntary admissions; but the number of patients in mental hospitals has fallen from 560,000 in 1955 to under 300,000 in 1974, while the number of hospital admissions has about doubled. If someone had predicted thirty years ago that most patients would voluntarily enter mental hospitals for treatment instead of being committed by the courts, he or she would have been thought an idle dreamer.

In the past madness has been surrounded by as much or more paleologic as punishment. Prejudice and discrimination against mental patients still exists, but they do not have the devastating impact that they did when mental patients were ostracized, exorcised, or locked up indefinitely. A sufficient amount of paleologic has drained away to enable former mental patients to be elected to office and occupy positions of trust and responsibility as well as to encourage the courts to strike down the remaining traces of discrimination.

Let us hope that the warehouse for convicts follows the warehouses for committed lunatics and for orphaned children into deserved oblivion. What was in each case proposed as a humane alternative was found to be ineffective and inhumane. This does not mean that we must return to the whip, the thumbscrew, and the gallows for criminals. While it can be argued that forty lashes for breaking the law are more humane than two years of imprisonment, the choice before society is not merely between various methods of aversive conditioning, it is between negative and positive reinforcement. As Philip Zimbardo points out, "all the psychological studies we have show you can always produce the same behavior using positive reinforcement that you can with negative reinforcement; that it is more lasting; that you don't have all the undesirable side effects of people disliking, hating, wanting to attack the person who uses the punishment." [8] The retribution model of handling offenders is simply too costly in terms of human lives. Fortunately, we do not use a vengeance model for madness. Instead we have a reasonably clear policy that mad people are to be put out of circulation until they are no longer a danger to other people. Until very recently, however, their incarceration was open-ended. A lunatic who had never hurt anyone could end up spending more time behind bars than a murderer or rapist. The reform of commitment laws has considerable relevance to reform of penal codes.

LPS Act

In 1969 the California Legislature passed the Lanterman-Petris-Short (LPS) Act to insure the rights of mental patients.[9] This act allows only three criteria for involuntary commitment to a mental hospital: danger to self, danger to others, and grave disability. A person brought to a mental facility involuntarily must be evaluated by the attending physician to see if he meets any of these three criteria. If he does, a physician can certify him and hold him for an additional seventy-two hours. The patient is also advised of his right to counsel and is permitted to make two telephone calls. After the seventy-two hours it takes two signatures, including one from a psychiatrist and one from another professional, to certify the patient for an additional two weeks. If at the end of this period a person is considered a danger to others—defined as presenting, as a result of mental disorder, an imminent threat of substantial physical harm to others and having threatened, attempted, or actually inflicted physical harm upon another—he may be recertified for an additional ninety days. At the time of recertification, there must be a court hearing during which it is the patient's right to request a jury trial on the question of whether he is imminently dangerous. This trial must commence within ten judicial days of the filing of the petition, unless the person's attorney requests a delay. At the court hearing and the jury trial, if the person has requested a trial, the accused is given all the rights and services of a criminal defendant, including a public defender and expert witnesses if he is indigent, and the right to cross-examine witnesses. If he is held for this ninety days, he must then be released unless the medical director of the hospital to which he has been sent files a new petition for certification on the grounds that the patient has threatened, attempted, or actually inflicted physical harm to another during the ninety-day period and still presents an imminent danger. If the hospital does file a new petition, another hearing is held in superior court. If the court determines that the patient is still imminently dangerous, he may be remanded to an intensive treatment facility for another ninety days, and so on.

A person who is brought in under LPS as suicidal for seventy-two hours' observation may be certified for two weeks and then recertified in the same manner for another two weeks, but after this he must be released. There is no legal way to hold him beyond a maximum of thirty-one days. The third category of commitment under LPS is the gravely disabled person who is unable to care for his basic requirements and is in need of care and supervision as a result of mental disturbance or chronic alcoholism. This person may be certified for two weeks beyond the initial three-day observation period, after which the court may appoint a conservator (usually a civil servant) to place the patient in an appropriate institution and keep track of him thereafter. Every conservatee has the right to a jury trial to determine whether or not he is gravely disabled. The patient can also petition for release every six months, and even if he does not, his case is automatically reheard at least once a year. The act also guarantees the involuntary patient's various legal and civil rights. In June 1975 the U.S. Supreme Court decreed that a mental patient could not be held involuntarily without treatment unless he was a danger to himself or to other people. This decision does not go as far as the California LPS in that it still leaves open involuntary commitment *with* treatment regardless of dangerousness and includes the provision of indefinite commitment for suicide risks.

A major outcome of the LPS Act was to transfer the burden of proof from the patient, to prove his sanity, onto the state, to prove his continued dangerousness before a jury of his peers. A person could no longer be committed to a mental hospital because he was "not mentally healthy" but only if he was proven to be a danger to himself or others. Establishing one's mental health is extremely difficult to do in any event, and virtually impossible if one resides in a mental institution. In Chapter 6, the imposture of David Rosenhan and several of his associates who had themselves admitted to mental hospitals by feigning insanity was described.[10] Once they were inside, they acted perfectly sane, but this was ignored or interpreted clinically by the hospital staff. Behavior that was perfectly normal and innocuous looked crazy in a mental hospital and behavior that was odd outside made a lot of sense in the crowded, dull institutional regime. How does one prove that one is mentally healthy in a crazy place? To question rules or procedures that are stupid or unnecessary brings an immediate diagnosis of paranoia or psychopathy. The customary definition of mental health has no meaning within the tight spaces of a total institution. Mental health is defined as:

> A relatively enduring state wherein the person is well adjusted, has a zest for living, and is attaining self-actualization or self-realization.[11]

The difficulty of proving mental health to a hospital board is obvious now, although it wasn't for over a century. Under LPS the state must prove that the inmate is a danger to himself or others before he can be committed. This has produced a dramatic drop in the number of commitments, since it is very difficult for the state to prove anything on the basis of the patient's behavior in hospital. There is also a tremendous burden on administrators of paperwork and court appearances if they try to commit patients. The result has been that many patients who would otherwise have been incarcerated were released. The courts took the position that if officials were unwilling or unable to prove that a patient was dangerous, a penalty as serious as the deprivation of liberty was unwarranted.

The LPS Act has not been without its critics. In the beginning the hostility came from hospital employees and officials who saw their institutions, jobs, and payrolls dwindling. More recently, criticism has come from correctional officials who claim that jails and prisons have become the dumping grounds for mental patients who refuse voluntary treatment. Reports began circulating about the increased number of mentally ill people in prison. The California State Employees Association, the group most affected by the mental hospital closures, declared that there "may be a correlation between the effect of LPS on mental health care in California and the recent violence in California prisons." [12] The director of the California Correctional System declared himself fully in support of efforts to keep the mentally ill out of his prisons. Several sheriffs gave belated recognition to the role that state hospitals had played in keeping undesirables off the streets. Assistant Sheriff William J. Anthony of Los Angeles stated, "It used to be we could find this guy exposing himself. We could take him to the county hospital for treatment and they would do him some good. We would probably never see him again. Now we have to throw him in jail. He gets out and does it again. Finally the judge gets tired of seeing him and sends him to prison." [13]

The frustration of law enforcement authorities who find their institutions becoming the repositories of people who used to be dumped elsewhere is understandable. However, the solution of reopening closed warehouses would be a step backwards. People warehouses are not needed, at least on the scale on which they were built in the halcyon institution days of the 1950s. The basic issue is not whether the warehouses are called prisons, mental hospitals, or detention centers, but their value to society. It has never been demonstrated that state hospitals are effective in dealing with people who expose themselves or with any type of sexual deviates. The closed society of the institution is often the very worst environment for these offenders. One can sympathize with the desire of sheriffs and wardens to get sex offenders out of prison, but hospital superintendents possess no magic cures. For many sex offenders a major overhaul of the morals laws would solve the problem at its source by getting the government out of the bedroom and the homosexual out of the public toilet. Homosexuals do not choose public restrooms for encounters because they are such attractive, interesting environments. Rather, they choose to make their contacts in restrooms because these are public places where a person's presence can be explained. The idea that former mental patients are responsible for prison violence betrays a woeful ignorance of schizophrenia. Incidents of violence in mental hospitals are rare; mental patients want to withdraw from the world, rather than attack other people. I have spent time on hundreds of psychiatric wards and have always felt safe, although somewhat uncomfortable, in the presence of so many isolated individuals. Group violence or organized escapes are unheard of on chronic wards. Mental patients do not engage in gang activities or the active illegal commerce found in prison.

The LPS Act illustrates the complexity of reform in a society with interconnected and overlapping institutions. It is not surprising that closing one type of warehouse will increase the pressure on other agencies engaged in storage operations. Fortunately the dramatic reduction in California's mental patient population has not resulted in a comparable increase in the prison population; most authorities credit the increase in the prison population from 20,000 in 1971 to about 25,000 in 1974 to tougher parole policies instituted as part of a law and order campaign.

If mental hospitals remain closed as prisons begin to close, it is likely that the next pressure point will be institutions for the retarded, which contain over 180,000 inmates. Class-action suits for adequate facilities and treatment for the retarded are already underway. As a result of one such suit, the U.S. District Court in Massachusetts awarded the Belchertown State School $2.6 million damages from the State for remodeling and other necessary improvements. If warehousing remains our major means of dealing with the severely retarded, it is likely that these institutions will become the dumping grounds for the mentally ill and the criminals. Organizations such as the American Association for Retarded Children will have to remain alert and politically active in order to resist these pressures to expand warehousing and indeed to channel them into the development of suitable noninstitutional programs.

I hope the implications of my comparison of mental hospital and prison reform are clear. I have *not* suggested that mental hospitals and prisons are identical in conception or purpose, or that the medical model is appropriate to corrections. Neither of these ideas is valid. There are great differences between the isolated schizophrenics and elderly people who make up most of the population of mental hospitals and the predominantly young, active, and almost protosocial inmates actively engaged in the prison economy. Nor is there a safe and effective medical treatment for criminality. My purpose in describing the reform of mental hospitals has been to illustrate a recent and relevant attempt to change a long-standing pattern of warehousing. Had we gone back in history a little further, we could have used the example of closing down warehouses for young children (orphanages).

I would not want to leave the impression that the reform of mental hospitals is concluded and that everything is rosy. Nothing could be further from the truth. Even in those states such as New York and California where the greatest progress at ending warehousing has been made, many problems remain in finding places in the community where lonely and isolated people can live productive lives with dignity, where the elderly are treated with respect, and people who are not too bright can find a niche in the economic system. We will have to develop means other than warehousing for handling people who have been defined as losers. This cannot be done through euphemism or administrative fiat. It will require programs, personnel, and public understanding. Knowing the failures as well as the successes of mental hospital reform, the criminal justice system is challenged to do better. Corrections departments have several years' lead time in anticipating and implementing institutional closure. If they do nothing and wait for the inevitable court orders, there will be the same economic and social dislocations that resulted from precipitous hospital closures. If they can plan ahead, community alternatives will be developed *before* rather than after existing prisons are shut.

DETENTION YES, IMPRISONMENT NO

11

Sing Sing Prison is doing hard times these days. Parts of Sing Sing look like a ghost town, boarded up and padlocked. Its inhabitants, for the most part, are transient prisoners awaiting trial in New York City courts—kept here on a makeshift basis only because the detention cells in the city are overcrowded.

Imprisoning offenders for long periods has failed as a social policy. It has shown itself to be costly, inhumane, and discriminatory. Even under the best of conditions (which rarely prevail) long-term confinement disrupts the fabric of human relationships a person develops over a lifetime. It has the most severe consequences for an inmate's family, who are the innocent victims of his or her incarceration. The arguments that psychiatrist Thomas Szasz directs against involuntary commitment to mental hospitals apply equally to the involuntary incarceration of offenders—the political nature of the process, the violation of civil rights, the inevitability of abuses in places hidden from public view, and the corrosive effects of the institutional routine upon everyone connected with it.[1] Such problems are inherent in any policy that deprives people of their liberty and places them in restricted surroundings for long periods under the absolute control of other people.

It is time to end the policy of warehousing people who break the law. There is a big difference between short-term storage and warehousing. People can be likened to merchandise that will spoil on the shelves if kept too long. It is necessary to have proper temperature control, adequate air circulation, and sufficient shelf space to prevent crowding, but these will only reduce the outward signs of deterioration. Even if we could freeze the contents into a state of suspended animation, people packages would depreciate. Thawed-out people aren't very good when the world outside and everyone else is two years older. The social and temporal disruption of imprisonment would remain even if we were able to minimize the possibility of damage during cold storage.

After examining the benefits and liabilities of imprisonment, Judge James E. Doyle concluded:

> I am persuaded that the institution of prison probably must end. In many respects it is as intolerable within the United States as was the institution of slavery, equally brutalizing to all involved, equally toxic to the social system, equally subversive to the brotherhood of man, even more costly by some standards, and probably less rational.[2]

The courts have taken the lead in expanding prisoner rights. A recent review of prison law states, "The burden has shifted from the affected person's having to establish why a practice should not be continued, to the administrator's having to justify why a particular practice should be followed."[3] There is every indication that the trend towards increased recognition of the inmate's civil rights will continue. I believe further that something like California's LPS Act would be extremely beneficial for prisoners. Although the specifics of the proposal are tentative, I would like to outline what the effect would be of transferring the burden from the offender to prove that he is not dangerous to the state to prove that he is dangerous.

An LPS Act for Corrections

Under an LPS type of act for corrections, short-term detention, up to six months, would still be used and would presumably retain its deterrent value. This will not significantly reduce the number of people incarcerated, since only a very small number of offenders actually end up behind bars. Sociologist John Irwin advocates short fixed sentences for every offender.[4] Given the unequal distribution of power and influence in this society, Irwin believes that any kind of discretion will mean longer sentences for street criminals than for white-collar criminals. While the idea of expanding the use of jail sentences deserves further scrutiny, it is pertinent to note that decreasing the length of sentences will not automatically reduce the number of inmates. Indeed, if everyone convicted of a crime were put behind bars for a fixed term, the number of people locked up would actually increase. The important question is whether this would have a greater deterrent effect upon crime than the current system, under which most offenders never see the inside of a jail and a few offenders serve incredibly long sentences.

It is always tempting to legislate exceptions to the rule. Our tax structure is full of such attempts. Yet it is not primarily the blind, the disabled, and the poor who benefit from tax loopholes, it is the wealthy. The obvious inequities have undermined the legitimacy of our entire tax system. Many authorities believe that a standard 11 per cent tax on all personal incomes would give the treasury the same amount of money it gets today and do it much more fairly. If assistance to the blind, disabled, or poor were given as a direct subsidy, it would not erode the legitimacy of the tax system. The notion of standardized anything seems simplistic at first hearing. Yet an understanding of the connection between power, law, and justice reveals that any deviation from standardization tends to benefit those groups who have the greater power and resources. If the federal government wants to assist a specific industry or region it can do this through subsidy or direct cash payment rather than resorting to an investment tax credit or 200 per cent depreciation. The more complicated the aid formula, the more likely it is to be manipulated by those who have the resources to hire the best lawyers and accountants. There are innumerable ways that inequalities in power and resources have made themselves felt in the criminal justice system. The consistent application of law and punishment will not by themselves help to redistribute income, but they will reduce the discriminatory consequences of the present imbalance.

Respect for the law is diminished when obvious offenders are not punished. According to sociologist Amitai Etzioni the infrequent, arbitrary, or half-hearted enforcement of moral precepts reduces the commitment among members of the community.[5] Punishment is important, not only to insure that "evil gets its just deserts," but to reaffirm society's collective agreement about what is right and what is wrong and to reinvigorate individual conscience. Next to nonenforcement of laws, the factor which contributes most to disrespect for law is the disparate and sometimes whimsical imposition of penalties, which has given rise to such pejorative terms as "bargain basement justice," "judge shopping," and "courthouse lotteries."[6]

Traffic accidents cost the nation $20 billion in 1973 compared to $5 billion for the direct cost of serious crimes. More than five times as many people were injured in traffic accidents as were hurt in rapes, robberies, and aggravated assaults. Drinking drivers kill and maim far more Americans every year than are injured by other criminals. However, drinking drivers rarely go to jail even when they injure or kill someone. The majority are set free with a fine or probation. The experience of Scandinavian countries has shown that mandatory jail sentences can act as a serious deterrent to drunken driving. In Norway a person will end up in jail if she is caught walking towards a car with keys in her hand and alcohol on her breath, and the penalty is jail—not passing Go and collecting $200, but jail. There is every indication that mandatory jail sentences would be a significant deterrent to drunken driving in this country. It would also bring a new class of people into the jails and thereby serve the cause of penal reform. The obvious forms of brutality are not going to occur if half the inmates are middle-class businesspeople and professionals, along with a few lawyers and legislators. It would also mean the end of the drunk tank as a dirty, smelly, overcrowded pit which would be closed quickly by humane officials if it existed in the local zoo.

Under an LPS Act for corrections, the offender sentenced to serve less than six months would be released at the specified time. If he were sentenced for the full six-month period, there would be a jury trial at the end of his fixed term. It would be up to the jury at that time to determine whether or not he presents a danger to society. If the jury finds that he does not, he is released. However, if they feel that he is still a danger, he is incarcerated for another six months, after which there will be another jury trial, another determination, and perhaps another six-month sentence, until finally a jury decides that the state is unable to prove the inmate's further dangerousness. The critical difference between this system and the present one is that the burden is upon the state to prove further dangerousness. Since this task is extremely difficult, and most expert opinion in this area is suspect, the state is probably not going to attempt to hold too many people beyond the initial six-month period.*

The threat of a half-year in jail would be enough to deter most potential lawbreakers and serving it would still avoid the personal and vocational disruption, the degradation, and the expense of long-term incarceration. Some of those who would not be deterred by the possibility of six months in jail have already demonstrated that they are not deterred by longer sentences either. A shorter period would at least keep us from throwing good money after bad. There will always be categories of offenders who are poorly served by a system of punishment. There are some individuals who might calculate that the murder

* It would be premature and presumptuous for a nonlawyer to work out all the ramifications of such a system. New procedures will have to be evolved regarding the admissibility of materials from previous trials. The proposed system requires that subsequent trials *not* be rehearings of the original charges but rather directed specifically to the issue of continued dangerousness based on all the available evidence. The development of suitable procedures that protect the rights both of convicted offenders and of society will require a considerable amount of legal and legislative work.

of a hated person is worth six months or even six years in jail. There will be individuals motivated by ideology who would assassinate a public official as a symbolic act. Experience has shown that the risks of a ten-year sentence or capital punishment are unable to deter some assassins. Often the ideological assassin is a highly unstable individual whom no deterrent can touch. People of diminished mental capacity can be handled under existing psychiatric commitment laws such as the LPS. Long-term imprisonment of dangerous individuals in order to incapacitate them can still occur under the jury provisions described earlier. If a man convicted of planting a bomb still manifests, after six months in jail, a continued commitment to anti-social activities, most juries would probably decide that he was one of the small number of offenders requiring further incarceration. This determination would be made semi-annually by a jury following an incapacitation model rather than retribution. Six months is not a magic figure. Perhaps nine months or a year would be preferable. Some time period is necessary that is long enough to permit the offender to calm down but short enough to avoid the disruption and corrosive effects of long-term imprisonment.

The distinction between short-term detention and long-term confinement is not the familiar call for euphemism; I personally don't care if correctional facilities are ever again renamed. It is more important to limit the amount of time inmates spend behind bars than to rename prisons "detention facilities." The distinction between short-term detention and long-term isolation is exceedingly relevant to the topic of prison violence discussed earlier. Another unsuccessful penal innovation was the prison-within-a-prison where violent offenders could be kept segregated from other inmates. Testifying in court, psychiatrist Bernard Diamond emphasized the critical difference between detention as a temporary expedient and its use as a long-term solution.[7] Diamond, consultant to various correctional agencies, originally had supported the idea of the prison-within-a-prison. It was supposed to reduce the scale of facilities for those inmates requiring special treatment, provide a better ratio of staff to inmates, give everyone a single cell, and make special programs available. Unfortunately this liberal conception became distorted when authorities used the "Adjustment Centers" as punishment facilities where inmates spent years in isolation. Diamond testified that he still accepted segregation "as a temporary emergency measure to deal with an inmate who cannot be tolerated because of violence in some other situation. But that temporary first step must not be the prison's primary instrument for coping with the violent inmate." This same political distinction between isolation as a short-term expedient and as a long-term solution applies to society's handling of lawbreakers in general. Where the short-term removal of an offender may be necessary and even desirable in some cases, long-term incarceration becomes counter-productive. We must avoid the foolishness that twice as much is always twice as good. There are many situations, imprisonment being one, where half as much is twice as effective.

One can immediately find flaws in this approach. What if an ideological offender admits his wrongdoing and states a desire to change but isn't serious? Assuming a significant number of the jury believes in his conversion, there probably isn't much that can be done except release him at the end of six months. Perhaps his antisocial attitudes will be reduced by this demonstration of trust, rather than increased during long-term incarceration; but the main reliance would be on establishing a society tending towards social justice and diminishing crimes of opportunity through an adequate police system. While the perfectly just society is a utopian notion, the idea of a society striving towards this end is not. If it should turn out that the ideological criminal reverted immediately to planting more bombs, this would undoubtedly influence the jury at his next trial. I do not pretend that this is an ideal method for handling this type of offender. I am afraid that there is no ideal method. One has to compare the overall effects of this approach with the alternatives in terms of justice, morality, and cost. It is not necessary that every revision of a bad system prove itself to be perfect. Instead we should ask two questions: Does it help us move towards a more just and humane society? and Is it better than the system we have now?

Lawyers and legislators recognize that it is impossible to write laws to cover every contingency. There will always be cases where, due to accident or deliberate deceit on someone's part, the innocent are convicted and the guilty go free. For the same reasons there will be some instances where punishments are too harsh and other times when they are too light. The complexity of modern society and human behavior allows no other conclusion. The inevitability of marginal cases is not inconsistent with the previous call for fixed, prompt, and certain punishment for every offender, providing that the punishments are not exceptionally severe and irreversible. The shortcomings of any system of justice are mitigated when punishment is brief, restrained, and subject to frequent review.

This proposal is not heedless of the public safety. The burglars, muggers, and rapists who may be released under an LPS kind of determination are also released under our present nonsystem. It is true that many of them will spend more than six months incarcerated, perhaps an average of three years behind bars. What has the public gained and lost during this three years of incarceration? About the only positive gain would be three years with the offender off the streets. This gain is short-lived. Against the three-year respite from the specific offender we have an individual worsened and embittered during time wasted at a state institution, the cost to the taxpayers for his direct support and possibly for his family, his lost wages and the taxes he might have paid, and the corrosive effects upon society of maintaining large warehouses dominated by violence and corruption. The protection that warehousing offenders offers to society is temporary at best, illusory in the long run, and probably negative in terms of the effects of incarceration upon the inmate, his family, the public treasury, and upon the guards and the other citizens directly and indirectly responsible for maintaining penal institutions. The gains to be derived from three-year sentences are found largely in the realm of retributive paleologic. If I permit paleologic to guide my thinking, I can say without hesitation that I don't want robbers and rapists back on the streets in six months' time. I don't want them back in twelve months or twenty-four months or thirty-six months. Quite frankly, I don't ever want to see them again. However, unless we go to capital punishment or life imprisonment, these people are going to be back on the streets. We are faced with the choice between several years of meaningless incarceration that is likely to embitter the offender even further, and brief detention to enable him to settle down and get over his anger while we put our money instead into restitution, job training, and work alternatives. The weight of logic is on the side of the short sentences with a jury trial mechanism for incapacitating individuals who are still dangerous. Paleologic keeps us punishing people beyond the point that logic tells us we are doing them and ourselves much good.

How About Those Wild Animals?

The hottest correctional issue today is what should be done about "the hardened criminal." I put this phrase in quotes because it is a simplistic notion. Many of these men and women were hardened by the years they spent in a succession of institutions intended to reform them. Today we are faced with the results of the shabby treatment of children, of young people pushed out of school, who are not wanted by society and who reciprocate through persistent criminal activities. The long-term solution is to change the society so that these unwanted, abandoned, and frustrated young people can lead lives with dignity. Imprisonment is primarily a youth problem in this society. Most people who end up in jail are between fifteen and thirty years of age. The process of entering this society even under the best conditions has many chaotic and tumultuous qualities. If one has been penalized and stigmatized from early childhood, one is likely to be set up for failure. I have heard the question about "the hardened criminal" asked in many forms.

> How do you deal with an incurable alcoholic?
> What can be done about the child who can't sit still?
> How about those incurable mental patients?
> What are you going to do about the habitual offender?

If the terms of the question are accepted unthinkingly, the answer is already there. A system built around failure predetermines the form of its institutions. If someone behaves like a wild beast—and incidentally most wild animals are very much afraid of people, but if this wild beast happens to go around slaughtering humans—then we will want to put him out of the way. But the fundamental difference between detention for short periods and permanent incarceration still holds. In the right kind of environment, alcoholics can be induced to stop drinking, drug addicts can go cold turkey or take a maintenance drug without becoming involved in a criminal culture, and "hyperactive children" can be induced to sit still. Visitors to Chinese schools claim that they never see hyperactive children and Chinese teachers don't understand the meaning of the term. By an odd coincidence, there were very few hyperactive children in the United States fifty years ago, but rather discipline problems that teachers dealt with behaviorally rather than medically.

It is unfortunate but true that there are violent people in this society. Some of them are in positions of authority and they don't get arrested. Others get into fights and end up in jail. For the latter sort of person we need an environment that provides a minimum of hassle. Most prison officials estimate that the number of inmates in need of continuous physical supervision is 10 to 15 per cent of the prison population. Previous studies have indicated that officials tend to overestimate the potential dangerousness of inmates, so this figure is probably on the high side. However, I don't think all the prison's problems have to be solved at one time. Let us proceed to empty the prison of the 85 to 90 per cent of inmates who are not "violent predatory offenders." This will provide a very different perspective on the remaining 10 to 15 per cent. The statements made by inmates during the Attica insurrection and in the letters from Soledad which came out during a brief hiatus in mail censorship revealed a restraint and dignity rare in human relationships. I do not want to romanticize the moral stature of the inmate population. I would, however, insist that it is false and misleading to characterize such people as wild beasts. For one thing, this locates failure within the individual rather than in the relationships between the individual and the environment. It also justifies existing power relationships by purporting to demonstrate that whoever succeeded must have had the right traits and those who failed lacked them. We will never solve the problem of the "hardened criminal" until we stop believing that criminality resides within the individual. People's actions are a response to the situations in which they find themselves. It is true that people differ in their responses to situations that are objectively similar, and sometimes the same individual responds in different ways to the same kind of situation, but in each case we are talking about transactions between the individual and the environment rather than either the individual or the environment in isolation.

The success of community alternatives for offenders has been dismissed by some critics as irrelevant to the problem of the "violent predatory offender." They believe that no matter how many community alternatives are developed for the "good inmate," there will always be some who require special institutions. This solution is terribly attractive to correctional officials and architects, who dream of the billions of dollars to be invested in new 200-man maxi-maxi institutions. However, before embarking on a new wave of prison construction, let us first rid our penal institutions of all those men and women who have not demonstrated a repetitive pattern of violent behavior and see how many are left. When it came time to close mental hospitals, it was surprising how many patients who were previously thought recalcitrant and intractable could be placed in boarding homes. The criticism that community placement programs are merely skimming the cream off the top suggests a different sort of experiment. Following a decompression period of six weeks, and with ample back-up staff and money, the population of the disciplinary wing of Attica could be released back into the community. This would require ample funds and staff for finding jobs, housing, transition expenses, and educational programs. There is reason to believe that the recidivism rate of this group of discharged inmates, particularly with ample back-up facilities, would actually be lower than that of other discharged criminals without adequate back-up services. This is not a visionary dream. Sol Chaneles developed Project Second Chance out of the general Attica population, although not specifically out of the disciplinary buildings.[8] Chaneles was able to demonstrate a much lower recidivism rate for inmates in the program than for other discharged inmates.

The period just after release is critical in determining whether or not the inmate will make it in society. Assistance during the transition back to society seems more important than job training, education, and therapy programs within institutions whose legitimacy and effectiveness are undermined by the coercive environment. The state will have to act as the employer of last resort to returned inmates. We cannot tolerate an economic system where large numbers of people are unemployed or marginally unemployed for long periods of their lives. If our present economic institutions cannot end chronic unemployment, we will have to find a system that will. Society has an eminently practical investment in seeing that ex-convicts have jobs upon release. For those inmates who do not have marketable job skills, there will have to be intensive training programs leading to real jobs. These programs already exist in the community and don't have to be duplicated in institutions. It doesn't take great prescience to guess where the money for these training programs, halfway houses, and jobs will come from. There must be a diversion of funds away from institutions and into community programs. Correctional employees will either adapt to working in the community or find their jobs abolished as institutions disappear. Billions of dollars are already going into a correctional system that doesn't work. It doesn't work because it relies on a method (imprisonment) that produces more problems than it solves.

What about the fellow who robs a grocery store for the sixteenth time? What is to be done about him? But, but, but, there are always buts. Somewhere during his youth, this fellow learned the wrong lessons in how to live. It isn't unlikely that he learned them from someone who had served time in the slammer, but this is a cheap answer. The grocery store robber must learn that this isn't a smart thing to do. This lesson is not going to be learned during five years in a totally criminal society. Instead of incarceration, this offender needs to find a more productive and less disruptive way of living. There are criminals in all social classes, but they are not the same sort. There are very few robbers and burglars in the middle or upper class. When people have decent jobs and living conditions, they don't go around robbing grocery stores. Then our problem is to see that they don't embezzle or cheat on taxes, but these are not crimes for which people spend time in prison. More often than not, society is willing to accept a restitution model for a white-collar crime but not for burglary.

For every horror story about a paroled ex-convict killing his estranged wife or robbing a supermarket, one can produce an equally frightening tale of youngsters raped in county jail and prison inmates beaten and murdered. Perhaps the only way of counteracting atrocity tales by one side is to recount atrocities by the other side rather than attempt to deny the existence or minimize the significance of the first. However, I have never liked scare tactics as a method of argument. The realization that there is no perfect approach to crime and punishment will help eliminate the smugness and self-righteousness that prevent rational decision-making. The anger of someone whose apartment has been burgled or whose wife has been assaulted is understandable. People need to be protected against violent crime in a very immediate way; but some of the methods that have been proposed for accomplishing this, such as a further arming of the citizenry, seem likely to increase violent crime rather than decrease it, and the elimination of constitutional safeguards in the interests of apprehending criminals will lead us ever closer to a police state.

There are problems in society that are more serious and costly than the habitual offender. Given our available knowledge and resources, it would seem more profitable to put our energies into prevention than try to "cure" this small group of losers. We must be concerned about the millions of socially inept, not-so-intelligent, infirm, and handicapped people who have no place in present-day America. The waste of human resources in this country is appalling. The financial cost of this waste may eventually be enough to topple the system. We push millions of children out of school into nothingness. The elderly live half-lives at home or in convalescent hospitals, yet we know that they could make a vital contribution to community life. We also know that people of extremely low intelligence can be trained to perform industrial tasks.[9] There are numerous adults whose social ineptitude does not suit them for high-powered jobs, who keep getting into trouble when too much is expected of them, who need guidance and support but not institutional care. It will take tremendous creativity, intelligence, and some money to improve the situation of the vast underclass of losers in slums, ghettos, barrios, and rural areas whom Michael Harrington has described as "the other America." [10] No one can understand the workings of the criminal justice system without taking notice of the caste and class division of American society. I do not know the extent to which the perpetuation of these divisions is a deliberate matter (i.e. consciously planned by those who profit from it), but its continuation diminishes the quality of life of all Americans. It seems apparent that many aspects of the welfare system are designed to maintain and perpetuate inequalities rather than eliminate them. It would be too far-ranging a detour to consider major economic and social reforms in this book; it has been a difficult enough task to focus specifically on the prison system without being diverted to the reform of the courts, the law, and other social agencies that directly affect imprisonment. These important topics deserve lengthy discussion in their own right rather than a quick look from the guard tower. The organic interrelationships between social institutions means that a change in any one of them will affect them all.

The problem of the habitual criminal cannot be denied, yet it must be understood in perspective. He kills and maims less than automobile accidents and steals less than what they cost; and we do not usually put drivers, even those arrested on felony drunken driving charges, behind bars. Eliminating the conditions that produce hardened criminals and making crimes of opportunity less easy will be helpful measures. Getting those inmates out of prison who don't belong there will help put the problem in numerical perspective. I am willing to reserve judgment on the need for new specialized institutions until we can rid our present institutions of people who don't need to be there and work to eliminate the conditions that produce people who live outside the law.

There are special problems connected with people who have grown dependent upon institutions designed to rehabilitate them. Every so often there is a newspaper report of an inmate who has spent forty or more years behind bars and doesn't want to leave. Such people will need, at least temporarily, places of sanctuary. These would be completely voluntary settings patterned after the cooperative farms of a century ago or today's Synanon communities. Some ex-inmates will be able to enter such places for short periods and then move out; while others may want to stay there for a long time. Halfway houses would be far preferable to dumping these men into the anonymous rooming houses populated by discharged mental patients. Fortunately, a considerable body of experience with halfway houses for prison inmates, run either by public agencies, by private foundations, or by ex-convicts, has developed. Under proper conditions a halfway house can be an extremely effective method for introducing the inmate back into society. Federal pre-release centers were opened in 1961 in New York City, Chicago, and Los Angeles, and afterwards in Detroit, Washington, and Kansas City. Each center accommodates approximately twenty federal inmates who are transferred there several months prior to their expected parole dates. Some of the centers are located in large boarding houses; others occupy parts of old hotels, scattered rooms in a YMCA, or storefronts. As a deliberate policy, all centers are located in neighborhoods with mixed land usage, racial integration, and good public transportation.

What Is To Be Done?

Most books on imprisonment conclude with a set of specific recommendations under such headings as Legislative Reform, Legal Reform, and Social Reform.* I feel much the same towards these lists as I do about the well-documented accounts of prison brutality. These stories need to be told, but since they have already been told numerous times, they don't have to be repeated here. It should be obvious that we need to end chronic unemployment, eliminate racism, and make greater efforts to integrate young people into society. We will have to hold our institutions responsible for their failures rather than allowing them to blame their clients. There will have to be speedier processing of those arrested, less discriminatory use of bail policies, revision of drug laws and morals laws, more control of handguns, less emphasis on violence in the media, and above all a more equitable society that doesn't stigmatize millions of young people as losers and keep them that way their entire lives. The courts must recognize that people do not lose their civil rights when they become convicts or ex-convicts. We will need to put money into transition programs, job training, housing allowances, and education. When we finally stop shutting men and women away in oppressive institutions for long periods, programs to help establish community ties afterwards will be unnecessary. Until then, we will still have to deal with two centuries of reliance upon imprisonment.

The legislative branch can do much to assist the trend to eliminate warehousing. In 1970 the Iowa Legislature passed Senate File 190, which gave authority to county boards of supervisors to designate any facility as a county jail and determine its administering agency.[11] As a result of this law, county boards could designate noninstitutional alternatives, such as halfway houses or a section of a YMCA, as a county jail to which sentenced offenders could be assigned. Some 80 to 90 per cent of the residents at the Des Moines alternative facility are either employed or engaged in training programs in the community.

* Excellent recommendations are presented in William Nagel, *The New Red Barn* (New York: Walker and Company, 1973); Giles Playfair and Derrick Sington, *Crime, Punishment, and Cure* (London: Secker and Warburg, 1965); and the National Advisory Commission on Criminal Justice Standards and Goals, *Report of the Task Force on Corrections* (Washington, D.C.: Government Printing Office, 1973).

More than 95 per cent of those employed work in private businesses rather than for the state or in government-supported programs.

Thomas Mathiesen distinguishes between positive reforms that aim at abolishing the present system and negative reforms that perpetuate it.[12] Absolute prejudgments of specific reform measures must be avoided. The tactical advantages and disadvantages of a particular measure must be judged in terms of a long-term strategy. Requiring a state to provide humane conditions of incarceration might produce modern pastel-hued prisons. The institution lobby would be pleased with this outcome. On the other hand, the same court decision could provoke taxpayer resistance to building expensive new facilities when the previous ones hadn't worked. This was the outcome of court decisions in Alabama requiring the state to meet a specified minimum of amenity and treatment in institutions for the insane. Unwilling to finance the required renovations and staff additions, the authorities chose to reduce the number of people incarcerated. The strategic implication of proposed reforms in the penal system and new lawsuits must be carefully considered to see whether or not they will perpetuate the system they are supposed to change.

The overhaul and improvement of our short-term detention facilities, notably city and county jails, is long overdue. As Goldfarb has documented, jails are the most neglected aspect of the correctional system.[13] No one is even sure how many jails exist in the nation—4000? 3500? 3000? One difficulty in getting an accurate count is that many temporary facilities, such as the storage room at a police station or the drunk tank in a local hospital, are considered jails in some reports and not in others. About half of the 160,000 daily occupants of jails are there solely because they were not able to post bond while awaiting trial. The physical amenities of most jails are deplorable, and they lack programs or recreational facilities. The end of long-term warehousing and a greater reliance upon short-term detention will increase the importance of jails. Middle-class drunk drivers sentenced to short mandatory jail terms would never tolerate the conditions that habitual drunks must accept. The end of warehousing will release money and personnel for improving, staffing, and renovating short-term detention facilities. In this book I have only touched in passing upon the reform of the courts, juvenile institutions, institutions for the retarded, drunk tanks, and jails. It would not have been possible to cover these other important topics except in the most superficial way. Replacing long-term incarceration with short-term detention for all except imminently dangerous criminals will have ramifications for all aspects of the criminal justice system.

Amnesty

Declaring the nation "at war" with crime, federal officials have called for an all-out assault on crime by any means available. A warfare state requires the suspension of certain constitutional safeguards, but the overall objective of war is to win. Once the enemy is beaten, then, it is said, the nation can resume worrying about luxuries such as individual rights. The enormous interest in security hardware reveals further traces of this warfare model. For the past two decades the military establishment has been training the police of other nations in counter-insurgency techniques. Programs in which the American military train American police have already begun. The SWAT program developed in Los Angeles—an acronym for Special Weapons and Tactics—was commissioned to "merge police and military strategies under those conditions requiring special tactics." Most SWAT members in Los Angeles are combat veterans, and SWAT training was originally done at the Marine Corps base at Camp Pendleton. Today SWAT police across the country keep abreast of current developments at the U.S. Army Research Institute at Fort Belvoir, Virginia.[14]

About the only hopeful feature of a warfare model is the concept of amnesty. We can declare that we have won the war on crime or that we have lost it; it doesn't matter, just so long as we can grant amnesty to all combatants. We can cease hounding men and women for offenses committed decades ago and stop using the power of the law to push people further into criminal activities. This is certainly the case with drug use, where the Harrison Act of 1914 transformed a medical illness into a crime. Our morals laws turn millions of Americans into criminals in their bedrooms. The war on crime has already seen the introduction of hidden cameras and microphones in public restrooms. The FBI has publicized this new application of technology as a means of reducing sexual perversion. As we overhaul our morals laws we can declare amnesty for previous offenders.

The American Constitution gives the President the power "to grant reprieves and pardons," which has been interpreted as including clemency in many forms:

> Full pardon, pardon to terminate sentence and restore civil rights, pardon to restore civil rights, conditional pardon, amnesty, amnesty on condition, reprieve, commutation, commutation on condition, and remission of fines and forfeitures.[15]

Numerous state, local, and federal codes and court decisions have used these terms loosely and often interchangeably. *Amnesty* literally is a forgetting of specific acts (cf. amnesia) and has traditionally been used to cover categories of individuals, while the term *pardon* (literally, to forgive) is used for specific individuals. However, even these terms have been used inconsistently. George Washington in 1795 granted a "full, free, and entire pardon" to the insurrectionists in the Whisky Rebellion; and in 1865, following the Civil War, President Andrew Johnson granted full pardon to most former Confederates who would take an oath of allegiance to the United States. Amnesty has been granted mainly for political and military offenses against the state, but on occasion it has also been applied to civil offenses. On December 24, 1952, President Truman pardoned all ex-convicts who served in the army more than a year during the Korean War. In 1975 the Soviet Union announced an amnesty on the thirtieth anniversary of World War II, to apply to all civil prisoners with a good war record. It is not clear just how many people were included in the Soviet proclamation, but the idea of linking amnesty for civil offenders to a national celebration can counteract the paleologic of retribution by transferring emotion from revenge into celebration and dedication to the future. Amnesty is a decision not to prosecute or punish further a class of citizens. In forgetting, amnesty does not consider guilt or innocence or whether or not a crime has ever been committed. Amnesty is a government decision not to apply a law under certain circumstances. It is usually granted after there has been a change in the political climate which, for very practical reasons, makes amnesty "more expedient for the public welfare than prosecution and punishment." Often used in the interests of social justice and reconciliation, it is the law's way of undoing what the law has done.[16]

If the public is to accept job training or other benefits for ex-prisoners of the war against crime, it will probably do it not on humanitarian grounds but as a matter of self-interest. The public will have to be shown that such programs will help reduce crime either directly or indirectly. This sort of appeal to self-interest is probably the best antidote to whatever paleologic cannot be drained away through public discussion. The precedent of aid to defeated opponents after the Second World War is relevant. The Marshall Plan and other aid programs were sold to the American public primarily as a matter of national self-interest and only secondarily as humanitarian measures. The aid programs succeeded to the extent that Germany and Japan gained economic power and became the United States' strongest allies. This can be contrasted with the aftermath of the First World War, when the victorious Allies took reparations instead of giving assistance, and the collapse of the German economy produced the conflagration of World War II.

Looking back through history, it is difficult to find an instance where amnesty has not *in retrospect* been regarded as a great success and vindictive retribution a terrible failure. The problem is how to convert this hindsight into foresight and drain away the paleologic of retribution so that rational assessment of future consequences can occur. The approach to punishment described here does not assume a totally rational human being—far from it, as evidenced in the lengthy consideration of paleologic. While nonrational components of punishment exist and color people's opinions, paleological thinking can and must be handled rationally. This will not be easy, and it cannot be done overnight.

The courts have traditionally interpreted amnesty to be an executive prerogative, either of a state governor or of the President. When the California Legislature in 1938 attempted to pardon labor leader Tom Mooney, the state attorney general declared that the bill was an unconstitutional invasion of executive pardoning powers. Separation of powers severely limits the ability of the federal government to declare a national amnesty for civil prisoners even if it wanted to. However, the federal government could declare amnesty for military prisoners and those in federal facilities, and, through its moral leadership, encourage state and county jurisdictions to do likewise. Serious abuses of the pardoning power have led to numerous attempts to curtail its use by the executive branch. However, the wisdom of allowing executive review when conditions change has usually led to a return of pardon, clemency, or amnesty in some form. The positive aspects of the pardoning power were forcibly stated in 1940 by Attorney General Homer Cummings: "The prerogative has always been near to absolute power and has been subject to abuse. At the same time it has been almost uninterruptedly within easy reach of the creative mind of mankind as a weapon to break the rigidity of law and custom and their resistance to progress and reform. When we weigh the abuses and errors of pardon against its social benefits, the scales tip definitely in favor of this old and ever-young institution." [17]

Desertion from the military in times of war used to be a serious crime, punishable by long imprisonment or death. Yet following almost every conflict in U.S. history, there has been a major program of amnesty, either conditional or full, for deserters and draft evaders. Desertion and evasion were punished, not by firing squad or prison, but by restitution or stigma, or forgotten in the interests of getting the offenders back into the mainstream of society. The success of these programs demonstrates how a restitution or forgiveness model can be used for what have previously been serious crimes. The desire of some segments of the public for further retribution was submerged in the general recognition of the need for national unity.

A proclamation of amnesty, either full or partial, would be a significant step toward ending the war on crime. We already apply the amnesty concept in some civil matters. The "no questions asked" campaigns for turning in handguns, conducted by police departments, often with a $50 bounty for each gun returned, is one application. The history of the gun and whether or not it came into the owner's possession legally are not considered. There is no punishment, but only a reward.

Such programs reveal a pragmatic concern with the future and downplay the past. They aim to get guns off the streets and deserters back into society with a minimum of fuss and bother. There is no reason why this approach could not work for other civil crimes, unless it is believed that robbing a grocery store is a more serious act than desertion from the military in time of war. Traditionally the penalties for desertion have been at least as high as those for robbery.

Conditional amnesty could get numerous offenders currently living outside the law back into the mainstream of society. A government program would not attract all civil criminals, but even if it reached several thousand people living worried lives under assumed names, it would be beneficial. A recent newspaper article described the case of a young Arkansas man who was eighteen years old in 1967 when he was convicted of a $200 burglary and sentenced to a ten-year prison term (!). The brutal conditions of the prison, for which fifteen officials were later indicted on forty-six federal counts, compelled the young man to escape. He hopped a freight to New Mexico, took on a new name, obtained a job, and married. He kept his past a secret from his wife because "he didn't want her to worry." Following the birth of his daughter in 1972, he made the mistake of calling his brother just to say hello. When the brother and his wife were divorced, the wife notified the FBI, who came and returned the young man to jail. The Arkansas corrections director admitted the model muddle he was in: "Here is a man who, so far as we know, is able to live on the outside.

. . . I am not sure what end would be served by keeping him a long period of time, but still we have laws that exact punishment for crimes." At the moment, the escapee is out on his own recognizance while decisions of the various administrative boards are moving him inexorably closer to prison.[18]

Crime is directly associated with age. The vast majority of people sent to penal institutions are between fifteen and thirty years of age. Psychopaths and people with a long history of antisocial activities, who are generally regarded as unchangeable by traditional psychotherapy, often reach an existential crisis in their thirties. The psychopath realizes that he has been on a one-way street traveling in the wrong direction, but his long criminal record, the conditions of parole, and perhaps pending charges prevent his return to the mainstream of society. The older convict or ex-convict who wanted to change his ways would benefit directly from an amnesty program. Not only would this be humane, it would be far less expensive and more effective in bringing offenders back into society than the programs currently in use. There are many applications of the amnesty concept within the criminal justice system. We can reduce the extraordinarily long sentences imposed upon the small number of losers who end up in prison. Some of the long sentences are due to arbitrary and discriminatory differences between districts in sentences imposed even for the same crime. Amnesty could also mean the shredding and recycling of police records, files, and dossiers over ten years old.

We are finally beginning to apply a sensible amnesty approach to heroin addiction. Ever since the Harrison Act of 1914, the nation has dealt with the problem by putting heroin addicts into jails or ineffective public hospitals. The availability of methadone and organizations such as Synanon have changed the situation. A judge at her discretion can assign a convicted drug offender to one of these programs instead of jail. There were still an estimated 724,000 heroin users in 1973 who accounted for over 150,000 arrests and many billions of dollars of drug-related crime. For the past fifteen years, Great Britain has tried a different approach, in which heroin addicts are able to register for maintenance doses. The success of the British program is seen in the plateau over the past five years in the number of registered addicts and the removal of organized crime from the drug trade. There is no profit for pushers, enforcers, and other segments of the criminal apparatus. This is not the place to compare heroin maintenance with methadone maintenance or with therapeutic communities. British clinics use all of these approaches, and no effort is made to force local treatment programs into a single mold. There are still serious problems with the British system. A study of 111 of the first 372 individuals receiving maintenance doses of heroin in British clinics revealed the program's shortcomings. Of this group, 36 per cent had received in-patient treatment for hepatitis, abscesses, and overdoses, and two-thirds of the group had been hospitalized for some drug-related problem. A sizable number had engaged in criminal activities in the preceding three months and only half were employed on a full-time basis.[19] During the beginnings of methadone programs in the U.S. there were problems with black market sale of the drug and with overdoses.

Similar difficulties are to be expected in any major overhaul of the criminal justice system. We have to be prepared for failure during the period of reconstruction. However, the failure must be judged not in absolute terms but relative to the record of the previous system. The British plan of heroin maintenance has shown a sixfold rise in registered addicts over the past fifteen years, from 437 in 1960 to approximately 2500 today. This is largely due to addicts coming out of the closet once they saw that the program was working. People living outside the law were justifiably suspicious of a program which required them to register. Amnesty in this case has meant officially substituting a legal addiction for an illegal one.

Such programs reveal a pragmatism absent in the way other offenders are treated. If we are going to develop a rational means of handling lawbreakers, we must insist on results in the future, and hold our institutions responsible for their records, rather than make them agents of vengeance for past misdeeds. An offender often views his crime as some kind of revenge in itself, either revenge upon society in general, upon merchants as a class, or upon his parents or schools—and society's revenge upon him sets in motion a continuing spiral of escalating retribution. Amnesty is one way out of this cycle, not for all offenders, but for many.

NOTES

CHAPTER 1

1. 1. W. H. Chatfield, *Prisons under sentence*. Surrey, Eng.: Chatfield Applied Research Laboratories, 1972.
2. G. de Beaumont and A. de Tocqueville, *On the penitentiary system in the United States and its application in France*. Carbondale: Southern Illinois Univ. Press, 1964.
3. A. H. Passow. Beleaguered institution. *The Nation,* December 14, 1974, pp. 623–26.
4. A. Etzioni, ''Alternatives'' to nursing homes. *Human Behavior,* April 1975, p. 10.
5. R. Clark, *Crime in America*. N.Y.: Simon & Schuster, 1970.
6. T. S. Szasz, *The age of madness: The history of involuntary mental hospitalization*. N.Y.: Anchor Press/Doubleday, 1974.

CHAPTER 2

1. M. Siegler and H. Osmond, *Models of madness, models of medicine*. N.Y.: Macmillan, 1974.
2. I. R. Kaufman, ''Are there two brands of justice?'' *Daily Democrat,* May 1, 1975, p. 8.
3. D. Glaser, *The effectiveness of a prison and parole system*. Indianapolis: Bobbs-Merrill, 1964.
4. S. Chaneles, Project Second Chance. *Psychology Today,* March 1975, pp. 44–46.

5. *Spain* v. *Procunier,* United States District Court, Northern District of California, Vol. 18, p. 2752.
6. J. Augustus, *A Report of the labors of John Augustus.* Boston: Wright and Hasty, 1852, p. 23.
7. S. C. Wee, "Singapore still flogs felons." *Sacramento Bee,* September 26, 1974, p. A13.
8. D. J. Rothman, Prisons: The failure model. *The Nation,* December 21, 1974, pp. 656–59.
9. R. McGee, A new look at sentencing, Part 1. *Federal Probation,* June 1973, pp. 3–8.
10. *Individual rights and the federal role in behavior modification.* Washington, D.C.: Government Printing Office, 1974.
11. C. J. Sitomer, Convicts "furloughed" to college campus. *Christian Science Monitor,* January 13, 1975, p. 4.

CHAPTER 3

1. S. Arieti, *Interpretation of schizophrenia.* N.Y.: Robert Brunner, 1955, p. 186.
2. J. Adelson, The political imagination of the young adolescent. *Daedalus,* Fall 1971, *100,* 1013–50.
3. *Attorney General's survey of release procedures. Volume 3: Pardon.* Washington, D.C.: Government Printing Office, 1939.
4. T. Morgan, The Rosenberg jury. *Esquire,* May 1975, p. 128.
5. J. Wolpe, *The practice of behavior therapy.* N.Y.: Pergamon Press, 1969.
6. R. A. McGee, A new look at sentencing, Part 2. *Federal Probation,* September 1974, p. 11.
7. H. A. Davidson, Psychiatry and the euphemistic delusion. *American Journal of Psychiatry,* 1953, 110 (4).
8. G. Orwell, *A collection of essays.* Garden City, N.Y.: Doubleday, 1954, pp. 162–76.
9. H. Osmond, personal communication.
10. A. C. Kinsey, W. B. Pomeroy, and C. E. Martin, *Sexual behavior in the human male.* Philadelphia: Saunders, 1948.

CHAPTER 4

1. U.S. Department of Justice, *Prevention of violence in correctional institutions.* Washington, D.C.: Government Printing Office, June 1973.
2. S. Kowch, A crying need for care beneath the prison dome. *Montreal Gazette,* November 30, 1974, p. 3.
3. D. Underhill, The shadow of southern history. *The Nation,* June 21, 1975, p. 750.
4. A. J. Davis, Report on sexual assaults in the Philadelphia prison system and sheriff's vans, mimeo. Philadelphia, 1968.

5. D. Rudovsky, *The rights of prisoners: An ACLU handbook.* N.Y.: Avon Books, 1973.
6. C. Haney, C. Banks, and P. Zimbardo, Interpersonal dynamics in a simulated prison. *International Journal of Criminology and Penology,* 1973, *1,* 69–97.
7. Cited in C. Haney and P. G. Zimbardo, The blackboard penitentiary. *Psychology Today,* June 1975, p. 106.
8. G. Jackson, *Soledad Brother.* N.Y.: Coward McCann and Bantam Books, 1970.
9. *Edwards* v. *Sard,* 250 F. Supp. 977, 981 (D.D.C. 1966).
10. R. G. Oswald, *Attica—my story.* Garden City, N.Y.: Doubleday, 1972.
11. J. B. Lieber, Gunfights in the graveyard. *The Nation,* January 18, 1975, pp. 32–47.
12. W. G. Nagel, *The new red barn.* N.Y.: Walker and Company, 1973.
13. Cited in Ramparts Editors, *Prison Life.* N.Y.: Harper Colophon Books, 1972, p. 15.
14. K. Burkhart, *Women in prison.* Garden City, N.Y.: Doubleday, 1972.
15. P. Blake, Race, homicide and the news. *The Nation,* December 7, 1974, pp. 592-93.
16. J. F. Steiner and R. M. Brown, *The North Carolina chain gang.* Chapel Hill: Univ. of North Carolina Press, 1927, p. 18.
17. Jackson, *Soledad Brother.*
18. A. Ferrante, Jail guards' suicides, union charges trigger Allmand investigation. *Montreal Gazette,* November 30, 1974, p. 5.
19. R. Sommer and B. A. Sommer, Corrupting the prisoners. *The New Republic,* July 20, 1974, p. 14.
20. N. Skelton, Prison was SLA recruiting office. *Sacramento Bee,* June 9, 1974, p. 1.
21. Lawyer supplied saw blades. *Sacramento Bee,* April 16, 1974, p. A4.
22. Night in prison shocks judges. *San Francisco Chronicle,* July 10, 1970, p. 2.
23. H. J. Steadman and J. J. Cocozza, *Careers of the criminally insane.* Boston: Lexington Books, 1974.
24. P. G. McGrath, Custody and release of dangerous offenders. In A. F. DeRuck and R. Porter, eds., *The mentally abnormal offender.* Boston: Little, Brown, 1968.
25. Cited in M. Grossman, Patients and victims. *Human Behavior,* July 1975, p. 8.
26. W. Coutu, *Emergent human nature.* N.Y.: Knopf, 1949.

CHAPTER 5

1. McGee, 1973, Part 1.
2. H. E. Thomas, Regressive maladaptive behavior in maximum security prisoners. Revised working paper for Conference on Prison Homosexuality, October 14–15, 1971.
3. Thomas, 1971.
4. D. O. Sumrall, Soledad. *American Correctional Officers Magazine,* 1971, 1 (3).
5. Jackson, *Soledad Brother.*
6. S. P. Smith, *American boys.* N.Y.: Putnam, 1975.

7. Oswald, *Attica—my story.*
8. F. S. Baldi, *My unwelcome guests*. Philadelphia: Lippincott, 1959, p. 13.
9. E. E. Flynn, Sources of collective violence in correctional institutions. In *Prevention of violence in correctional institutions*. Washington, D.C.: U.S. Department of Justice, LEAA, June 1973.
10. T. Murton and J. Hyams, *Accomplices to the crime*. N.Y.: Grove Press, 1969.
11. A. D. B. Clarke and B. F. Hermelin, Adult imbeciles, their abilities and trainability. *The Lancet,* August 13, 1955, pp. 337–39.

CHAPTER 6

1. G. Bermant, M. McGuire, W. McKinley, and C. Salo, The logic of simulation in jury research. *Criminal Justice and Behavior,* 1974, *1,* 224–33.
2. G. A. Mihram, *Simulation: Statistical foundations and methodology*. N.Y.: Academic Press, 1972.
3. M. Sherif and C. W. Sherif, *Groups in harmony and tension*. N.Y.: Harper, 1953.
4. C. E. Osgood, *An alternative to war or surrender*. Urbana: Univ. of Illinois Press, 1962.
5. P. G. Zimbardo, C. Haney, W. C. Banks, and D. Jaffe, A Pirandellian prison: The mind is a formidable jailer. *New York Times Magazine,* April 8, 1973, pp. 38–40.
6. C. Haney, C. Banks, and P. Zimbardo, Interpersonal dynamics in a simulated prison. *International Journal of Criminology and Penology,* 1973, *1,* 69–97.
7. Cited in Nagel, *The new red barn.*
8. I. J. Orlando, The mock ward. In O. Milton and R. Wahler, eds., *Behavior disorders*. Third ed. Philadelphia: J. B. Lippincott, 1973, pp. 162–70.
9. W. Caudill, *The psychiatric hospital as a small society*. Cambridge: Harvard Univ. Press, 1958.
10. L. Humphreys, *Tearoom trade*. Chicago: Aldine, 1970.
11. S. Cavan, *Liquor license*. Chicago: Aldine, 1966.
12. G. L. Kirkham, Doc Cop. *Human Behavior,* May 1975, p. 19.
13. D. L. Rosenhan, On being sane in insane places. *Science,* 1973, *179,* 250–58.
14. H. Leiderman, H. J. Mendelson, D. Wexler, and P. Solomon, Sensory deprivation. *Archives of Internal Medicine,* 1958, *101,* 389–95.

CHAPTER 7

1. C. Davis, Lord Jimmy. *Esquire,* March 1975, p. 146.
2. P. Berrigan, *Prison journals of a priest revolutionary*. N.Y.: Holt, Rinehart and Winston, 1970.
3. T. Wicker, cited in *The Outlaw: Journal of the Prisoners Union,* March–April 1975, p. 7.
4. G. E. Dickinson, Communication policies in state prisons for adult males. *Prison Journal,* 1972, *52,* 13–19.

5. M. T. Kaufman, Reporter's notebook: Attica trial something of an anticlimax. *New York Times,* March 30, 1975, p. 35.
6. Up the flag pole. *Time Magazine,* March 5, 1973.
7. H. Osmond, Our models and the law: A fascinating example misunderstood? Unpublished note, March 3, 1973.
8. P. V. Murphy, Our disgraceful system of combatting crime. *Reader's Digest,* February 1974, pp. 169–76.
9. S. Raab, Plea bargains resolve eight of ten homicide cases. *New York Times,* January 27, 1975, p. 39.
10. A. Hassler, *Diary of a self-made convict.* Chicago: Henry Regnery, 1954.
11. R. J. Ostrow, Saxbe urges citizen study of judges. *Sacramento Bee,* December 6, 1974, p. A21.
12. L. Meyer, U.S. prisons discard "rehabilitation for all" policy. *Washington Post,* April 13, 1975.
13. McGee, 1973, Part I.

CHAPTER 8

1. J. Mitford, *Kind and usual punishment.* N.Y.: Knopf, 1973.
2. W. Sage, Crime and the clockwork lemon. *Human Behavior,* September 1974, pp. 16–25.
3. I. P. Pavlov, *Conditioned reflexes.* London: Oxford Univ. Press, 1927.
4. J. B. Watson and R. Rayner, Conditioned emotional reactions. *Journal of Experimental Psychology,* 1920, *3,* 1–14.
5. B. F. Skinner, *The behavior of organisms.* N.Y.: Appleton-Century-Crofts, 1938.
6. K. Breland and M. Breland, A field of applied animal psychology. *American Psychologist,* 1951, *6,* 202–4.
7. O. R. Lindsley, Studies in behavior therapy: Status report 3. Waltham, Mass.: Metropolitan State Hospital, 1954.
8. J. Asher, "Behavior Mod" defiled. *APA Monitor,* 1974, *5,* 9–10.
9. H. J. Eysenck, The nature of behavior therapy. In H. J. Eysenck (ed.), *Experiments in behavior therapy.* Oxford: Pergamon Press, 1964.
10. R. W. Ramsay, The role of behavior therapy in psychotherapy. Lecture at the Univ. of Amsterdam, September 13, 1971.
11. T. Ayllon and N. Azrin, *The token economy.* N.Y.: Appleton-Century-Crofts, 1968.
12. H. L. Cohen, J. Filipczak, and J. Bis, *Case 1: An initial study of contingencies applicable to special education.* Silver Spring, Md.: Education Facility Press, 1966.
13. E. L. Phillips, E. A. Phillips, D. Fixsen, and M. M. Wolf, Behavior shaping works for delinquents. *Psychology Today,* June 1973, pp. 75–79.
14. T. Ayllon and J. Michael, The psychiatric nurse as a behavioral engineer. *Journal of the Experimental Analysis of Behavior,* 1959, *2,* 323–34.

15. Ayllon and Azrin, 1968.
16. Cohen, 1966.
17. J. McKee, Applied behavioral analysis and the imprisoned adult felon/Project 1: The cell block token economy. Available from Rehabilitation Research Foundation, P.O. Box 3587, Montgomery, Ala. 36109.
18. S. Geller, cited in *APA Monitor,* February 1975, p. 10.
19. S. Trotter, ACLU scores token economy. *APA Monitor,* August 1974, p. 7.
20. S. Trotter, Patuxent: "Therapeutic" prison faces test. *APA Monitor,* May 1975, p. 1.
21. C. Holden, Butner: Experimental U.S. prison holds promise, stirs trepidation. *Science,* August 2, 1974, pp. 423–26.
22. Trotter, August 1974.
23. S. Trotter, Token economy program perverted by prison officials. APA Monitor, February 1975, p. 10.
24. M. Knight, Child molesters try shock cure. *New York Times,* May 21, 1974, p. 43.
25. R. E. Sweet, Smokers get a shock. *Sacramento Bee,* July 18, 1971, p. A10.
26. S. Trotter and J. Warren, Behavior modification under fire. *APA Monitor,* April 1974, p. 4.
27. R. E. Sweet, Smokers get a shock. *Sacramento Bee*. July 18, 1971, p. A10.
28. Holden, 1974.
29. *Spain* v. *Procunier,* p. 2780.

CHAPTER 9

1. C. B. Hopper, *Sex in prison*. Baton Rouge: Louisiana State Univ. Press, 1969.
2. D. P. Jewell, Mexico's Tres Marias penal colony. *Journal of Criminal Law, Criminology, and Police Science,* 1958, *48,* 410–13.
3. W. D. Leeke, Prevention and deterrence of violence in correctional institutions. In *Prevention of violence in correctional institutions*. Washington, D.C.: U.S. Department of Justice, LEAA, June 1973.
4. Flynn, 1973.
5. Glaser, 1964.
6. D. Clemmer, *The prison community*. N.Y.: Rinehart, 1958.
7. G. Sykes, *The society of captives*. Princeton: Princeton Univ. Press, 1958.
8. E. Goffman, Characteristics of total institutions. In *Symposium on preventive and social psychiatry*. Washington, D.C.: Government Printing Office, 1958.
9. S. Zuckerman, *The social life of monkeys and apes*. N.Y.: Harcourt and Brace, 1932.
10. B. Bettelheim, Individual and mass behavior in extreme situations. *Journal of Abnormal and Social Psychology,* 1943, *38,* 417–52.
11. V. E. Frankl, *Man's search for meaning*. N.Y.: Washington Square Press, 1963.

CHAPTER 10

1. Goffman, 1958.
2. A. Etzioni, Interpersonal and structural factors in the study of mental hospitals. *Psychiatry,* 1960, *23,* 13–22.
3. A. Deutsch, *The mentally ill in America.* N.Y.: Columbia Univ. Press, 1946.
4. D. L. Dix, *On behalf of the insane poor.* N.Y.: Arno Press, 1971.
5. Siegler and Osmond, 1974.
6. H. B. M. Murphy, B. Pennee, and D. Luchins, Foster homes: The new back ward? *Canada's Mental Health,* September–October 1972.
7. B. Haslett, Jailhouse law. *Los Angeles Times,* October 9, 1974, p. 12.
8. *Spain* v. *Procunier,* p. 2826.
9. State of California—Human Relations Agency, *California mental health services act,* 1971.
10. Rosenhan, 1973.
11. H. B. English and A. C. English, *A comprehensive dictionary of psychological and psychoanalytical terms.* N.Y.: Longmans, Green, 1958.
12. G. Williams, Mental patients wind up in prison. *Sacramento Bee,* April 20, 1975, p. P1.
13. Williams, 1975.

CHAPTER 11

1. T. S. Szasz, *The second sin.* N.Y.: Anchor Press/Doubleday, 1974.
2. Judge James E. Doyle, 340 F. Supp. 544, 548–49, Western District, Wis. 1972.
3. South Carolina Department of Corrections, *The emerging rights of the confined.* Columbia, S.C.: The Correctional Development Foundation, 1972.
4. J. Irwin, Talk presented at Prison Symposium, Univ. of California, Davis, on November 16, 1974.
5. A. Etzioni, Anemic laws and activist antidotes. *Human Behavior,* March 1975, p. 6.
6. McGee, 1973, Part I.
7. Cited in *Spain* v. *Procunier,* p. 2699.
8. Chaneles, 1975.
9. Clarke, 1955.
10. M. Harrington, *The other America.* N.Y.: Macmillan, 1962.
11. *A handbook on community corrections in Des Moines.* Washington, D.C.: U.S. Department of Justice, LEAA, 1974.
12. T. Mathiesen, *The politics of abolition.* N.Y.: John Wiley, 1974.
13. R. Goldfarb, *The ultimate ghetto.* N.Y.: Anchor Press/Doubleday, 1975.
14. L. Remer, SWAT: The police berets. *The Nation,* May 24, 1975, pp. 627–28.
15. W. H. Humbert, *The pardoning power of the president.* Washington, D.C.: American Council on Public Affairs, 1941, p. 21.

16. A. Schardt, W. A. Rusher, and M. O. Hatfield, *Amnesty?* Lawrence, Mass.: Sun River Press, 1973.
17. *Attorney General's survey of release procedures,* Washington, D.C.: GPO, 1939.
18. Fugitive's dream fades. *Sacramento Bee,* March 19, 1975, p. A17.
19. G. V. Stimson, *Heroin and behavior: diversity among addicts attending London clinics*. N.Y.: Wiley, 1973.

NAME INDEX

Adelson, J., 36, 197
Anthony, W., 167
Arieti, S., 36, 197
Asher, J., 200
Augustus, J., 24, 197
Ayllon, T., 126, 127, 140, 200, 201
Azrin, N., 126, 127, 200, 201

Baldi, F., 75, 199
Bandura, A., 129
Banks, C., 53, 199
Beaumont, G. de, 196
Beccaria, C. B., 29
Bentham, J., 29
Bermant, G., 86, 199
Berrigan, P., 67, 104, 113, 199
Bettelheim, B., 151, 201
Blake, P., 198
Bohanon, L., 62
Breland, K., 124, 200
Breland, M., 124, 200
Brown, R., 63, 198
Burkhart, K., 62, 198

Caudill, W., 96, 199
Cavan, S., 96, 199
Chaneles, S., 182, 196, 202
Chatfield, H., 196
Clark, R., 13, 78, 109, 196
Clarke, A., 199
Clemmer, D., 148, 201
Cocozza, J., 67
Cohen, H., 126, 127, 200, 201
Cohen, M., 67, 113
Coutu, W., 69, 198
Cummings, H., 191

Darwin, C., 6
Davidson, H., 43, 197
De Freeze, D., 65
Deutsch, A., 155, 202
Diamond, B., 176
Dickens, C., 81
Dickinson, G., 107, 199
Dix, D., 8, 155, 202
Doyle, J., 172, 202

Ervin, S., 32
Etzioni, A., 11, 155, 174, 196, 202
Eysenck, H., 125

Flynn, E., 76, 199, 201
Frankl, V., 151, 201
Franklin, B., 4

Geller, S., 127, 132, 201
Glaser, D., 146, 196, 201
Goffman, E., 148, 154, 201, 202
Goldfarb, R., 187, 202
Gregory, R., 67
Groder, M., 136
Grossman, M., 198

Haney, C., 53, 198, 199
Harrington, M., 184, 202
Hassler, A., 113, 200
Hermelin, B., 199
Hill, J., 52
Hoffa, J., 67, 103, 113
Holden, C., 201
Holder, W., 46
Hopper, C., 201
Humburt, W., 202
Humphreys, L., 96, 199

Irwin, J., 173, 202

Jackson, G., 55, 63, 73, 198
Jewell, D., 201
Johnson, A., 189

Kandel, A., 129
Kaufman, I., 17, 196
Kinsey, A., 49, 197
Kirkham, G., 96-97, 199
Krasner, L., 125
Kunstler, W., 109

Leeke, W., 201
Lei, Q., 25
Leiderman, H., 99, 199
Lemmon, J., 19
Lieber, J., 60, 198
Lindsley, O., 125, 200
Luciano, L., 103

MacCormick, A., 92
MacDonald, J., 68
McGee, R., 118, 119, 197, 198, 200, 202
McGrath, P., 68, 198
McKee, J., 127, 201
Maddox, L., 54
Martin, J., 78
Mathiesen, T., 187, 202
Menninger, K., 8, 154
Mihram, G., 199
Mitford, J., 8, 78, 122, 200
Mooney, T., 191
Murphy, H., 202
Murphy, P., 111, 200
Murton, T., 77, 199

Nagel, W., 61, 186, 198, 199
Nightingale, F., 152

Orlando, I., 93-95, 199
Orwell, G., 45, 197
Osgood, C., 88, 199
Osmond, H., 17, 45, 110, 196, 197, 200, 202
Oswald, R., 58, 74, 198, 199

Passow, A., 196
Pavlov, I., 121, 123, 200
Pernasilice, C., 52
Playfair, G., 186

Raab, S., 200
Ramsay, R., 125, 135, 200
Rayner, R., 200
Remer, L., 202
Rosenhan, D., 98, 166, 199, 202
Rothman, D., 27, 197
Rudovsky, D., 198

Sage, W., 122, 200
Saunders, A., 129, 131
Saxbe, W., 116
Schardt, A., 203
Sherif, C., 87, 199
Sherif, M., 87, 199
Siegler, M., 196, 202
Sington, D., 186
Skinner, B., 121, 124, 130, 200
Smith, S., 73, 198
Sommer, B., 198
Sommer, R., 198
Steadman, H., 67
Steiner, J., 63, 198

Stimson, G., 203
Sumrall, D., 198
Sykes, G., 148, 201
Szasz, T., 15, 171, 196, 202

Thomas, H., 72, 198
Tocqueville, A. de, 196
Trotter, S., 201
Truman, H., 189

Underhill, D., 197

Wardrip, G., 109
Washington, G., 189
Watson, J., 121, 124, 200
Wells, W., 52
Wicker, T., 105, 199
Wolfe, M., 126, 200
Wolpe, J., 41, 197

Zimbardo, P., 53, 89-94, 98, 100, 139, 164, 198, 199
Zuckerman, S., 150, 201

SUBJECT INDEX

Abortion, 42
ACLU, 53, 129, 132, 134
Ad hocism, 19
Adjustment Center, 47, 177
Alcoholism, 135
Amnesty, 188-95; in Soviet Union, 189
Argot, 44

Baxtrom v. *Herold,* 67
Behavior modification, 31, 32, 121-41
Brainwashing, 31

China, 117
Cigarette smoking, 133, 135
Classical conditioning, 123
College volunteers, 162
Conjugal visiting, 9, 144
Corrections, def., 24
Courts, 17, 40, 41, 108; in Cuba, 109
Crime insurance, 28
Criminal insanity, 67

Davis Report, 52, 197
Desensitization, 41-42
Desertion, military, 191
Detention, def., 29
Deterrence, 20-22
Dispositional hypothesis, 53, 91
Drugs, 26; experiments with, 122, 128, 130; heroin, 193-94; laws on, 155; marijuana, 42
Drunk driving, 174, 187
Dysphemism, 45

Edwards v. *Sard,* 198
Elitism, 81
Euphemism, 42-50

Failure model, 27
Flogging, 25, 26
Formalization, 87

Gangs, 52, 57, 60, 63, 69, 87, 168
Guards, 71-84, 158
Gun control, 39, 40, 42, 192

Heroin addiction, 193-94; in Great Britain, 194; and Harrison Act, 189
Homicide, 68; arrests for, 111
Homosexuality, 59
Hyperactive children, 180

Idealism, 11, 53-57
Impersonations, 87, 95-101
Incapacitation, 21, 29-31
Indeterminate sentence, 13, 23, 26, 118; in Denmark, 13
Integration, 33-34

Jailhouse lawyers, 161
Jury deliberations, 86

Lanterman-Petris-Short Act, 164-79
LEAA, 12, 147

Mental health, 166
Mental hospitals, 14, 15, 154-170; Alabama, 187; Belchertown, Mass., 169; Broadmoor, 68; Elgin, Ill., 93; Mendocino, Ca., 160; Saskatchewan, 160
Mental retardation, 169, 184
Methadone, 193
Model, def., 19
Muslims, 161

Nazi camps, 140, 150
NIMH, 156
Norway, 174
Nursing homes, 11

Paleologic, 35-42, 163
Pardon, 189
Parole, 43
Penitentiary, 4
Plea bargaining, 110-12
Political prisoners, 82-84
Pre-release centers, 185
Prisoners Union, 45, 46, 130, 149
Prison lobby, 158
Prisons and jails: Allenwood, Pa., 13, 103-20; Arkansas, 76, 192; Atmore, Ala., 51; Attica, N.Y., 61, 109, 180, 182; Auburn, N.Y., 4, 5, 58; Bridewell, 3; California, 51, 167; California Medical Facility, 106, 128; Canada, 50, 64; Dannemora, N.Y., 103; Draper (Ala.) Correctional Center, 127; Ft. Worth, Texas, 114; Framingham, Mass., 114; Great Britain, 66; Hawaii, 57; Holman, Ala., 52; Jackson, Mich., 51; Leavenworth, Ks., 44, 161; Lewisburg, Pa., 13, 105, 113; Lompoc, Ca., 103-20; Lucasville, O., 57; Marion, O., 136; Mecklenburg, Va., 127, 132; Mexico, 145; Minnesota, 149; Muncie, Ind., 62; Nevada, 66; North Carolina, 63; Oklahoma, 55, 62; Oregon, 162; Parchman, Miss., 144; Patuxent, Md., 129; Philadelphia, 52, 61; San Quentin, 50, 55, 64, 105, 154; Singapore, 25; Soledad, Ca., 180; Somers, Conn., 133; Springfield, Mo., 129; Statesville, Ill., 62; Susanville, Ca., 158; Texas, 55; Walla Walla, Wash., 51; Walnut Street, Phila., 4, 5, 148
Probation, 24, 43; Iowa plan, 33; subsidy plan (Ca.), 33
Project Second Chance, 182
Psychopaths, 54, 58-59
Psychosurgery, 122, 130
Public service alternatives, 28, 149; in Portland, 28

Quakers, 3, 4, 6, 8, 23, 58, 67, 68, 107

Racism, 58, 61-64
Rape, 39, 52
Realism, 54
Recidivism, 21, 37, 182
Re-education, 31-33
Reform, 24-25
Reformatory, 24
Rehabilitation, 22-24, 116-19
Relocation, 29
Repentance, 32
Replications, 87
Research, 142-53
Restitution, 27-29, 38, 191; in Great Britain, 28; in New Zealand, 28
Retribution, 25-27, 38-42, 164
Riots, 51. *See also* specific prisons

Schizophrenia, 36, 125
Self-mutilation, 50
Sensory deprivation, 148
Sex offenses, 189
Silent system, 4, 5. *See also* Prisons and jails, Auburn
Simulation, 85-101
SLA, 65

Solitary confinement, 4, 5, 23, 148
Soviet Union, 15, 27, 31-32, 117
Spain v. *Procunier,* 197, 202
START, 129, 134, 137
Suicide, 50, 165
Surveys, in corrections, 146
SWAT, 188
Synanon, 136, 137, 185, 193

Territoriality, 59
Time perspective, 139
Tinsits, 69
Token economy, 126-32
Traffic accidents, 174

Violence, 50-70

Warfare model, 188
Watergate inmates, 102-20

Youth and crime, 193

Zoo, and research, 149-50